50
WAYS YOU CAN BE
PRO-LIFE

Tony Campolo
& Gordon Aeschliman

INTERVARSITY PRESS
DOWNERS GROVE, ILLINOIS 60515

InterVarsity Press® is the book-publishing division of InterVarsity Christian Fellowship®, a student movement active on campus at hundreds of universities, colleges and schools of nursing in the United States of America, and a member movement of the International Fellowship of Evangelical Students. For information about local and regional activities, write Public Relations Dept., InterVarsity Christian Fellowship, 6400 Schroeder Rd., P.O. Box 7895, Madison, WI 53707-7895.

All Scripture quotations, unless otherwise indicated, are from the HOLY BIBLE, NEW INTERNATIONAL VERSION®. NIV®. Copyright ©1973, 1978, 1984 by International Bible Society. Used by permission of Zondervan Publishing House. All rights reserved.

Cover illustration: Paul Turnbaugh

ISBN 0-8308-1394-2

Printed in the United States of America ∞

Library of Congress Cataloging-in-Publication Data
Campolo, Anthony.
    50 ways you can be prolife/Tony Campolo & Gordon Aeschliman.
      p.   cm.—(50 ways series)
    Includes bibliographical references.
    ISBN 0-8308-1394-2
    1. Voluntarism—Religious aspects—Christianity.   2. Social
service—Religious aspects—Christianity.   3. Volunteer workers in
social service—United States.   4. Birth control—Religious aspects—
Christianity.   5. Church and social problems—United States.
I. Aeschliman, Gordon D., 1957- . II. Title. III. Title: Fifty
ways you can be prolife. IV. Series.
HN49.V64C36   1993
361.3'7—dc20   92-46221
                                            CIP

17	16	15	14	13	12	11	10	9	8	7	6	5	4	3	2	1
06	05	04	03	02	01	00	99	98	97	96	95	94	93			

For the Love of Life . . .

. . . .

To be Christian is to love life. Those of us who have found a home in Jesus have also found a home with the author of all that lives. The Scriptures give us wonderful pictures of God creating, taking delight in his work.

We cannot really understand the mind and heart of the one who rules over the vast universe. We are amazed to peek in at the personal attention he gives to the work of his hands—"I knew you before you were formed in your mother's womb," "I know the number of hairs on your head," "I know every time a baby sparrow falls from its nest." Hymn writer Maltbie Babcock puts it thus:

This is my Father's world,
And to my listening ears

All nature sings, and round me rings
The music of the spheres.
This is my Father's world:
I rest me in the thought
Of rocks and trees, of skies and seas—
His hand the wonders wrought.

To the Christian, life is not an accidental explosion or random ordering of molecules. It is the miracle and evidence of God. Columnist George Wills says that the delicate layer of skin around a grape is proof enough to him that God exists. Agreed!

As we worship the Creator and admire the details of his artistry, we also weep from the pain of a canvas slashed by the work of evil. Just as we cannot understand the personal attention God gives to creation, we cannot perceive the awful pain God experiences over the ravages of creation. Abortion, rape, war, famine, racism, poverty—all of these are assaults on the perfect work of God's hands, assaults on the human spirit. Indeed, the earth groans.

But we do not faint. We live with the certain hope that in the final days the Lord will rescue all those who suffer. And in the days between now and that final hour we accept the privileged task of serving as angels of mercy wherever evil draws a line of battle against life.

As the authors, we hope you will find *50 Ways You Can Be Prolife* helpful as you live to celebrate our Creator and Friend. You will find that we have taken in the full sweep of life with these ideas—ways to defend the baby in the womb, ideas for educating youth on sexuality, means to care for people with AIDS, resources for loving the prisoner and caution regarding the malicious use of our tongues. This book is not intended to bolster the ideological debate about abortion. Other texts do a wonderful job of calling us to moral judgments in a day that devalues life. This book is a call to redemptive action in every arena of life. It is for people who want to get on with it! For people who love the Author of life and are ready to make a difference in the world.

We hope you will join us.

I

Organize for Life

• • • • • • • • • • • • • •

1

Life Excellence Committee

. . . .

A group of Christians in a rural western town decided to join their efforts in an attempt to influence their community toward biblical values in sexuality. There are eight churches in the town. A special meeting was called for lay activists from each church to discuss the value of bringing their prolife efforts into a unified team. The idea was a hit. This group of motivated individuals call themselves the "Life Excellence Committee." They're on a mission, to be sure, and they believe that their unified front will reverse the impact of secular sexual values upon their youth. They are probably right.

Every month committee members meet in a home to discuss their duties. Activities include reviewing video resources that educate youth on the consequences of an untamed sexual lifestyle, praying for the town, discussing ways to influence the local school board as it makes a decision on sexuality curriculum, and organizing public events that call for a return to biblical standards in lifestyle.

The name "Life Excellence" was chosen to cast a positive light on their ministry. They are not so much "against" something as they are "for" something—a higher quality of life based on a conviction that God's ways are without question the most excellent of ways.

We think these farmers are onto something.

Our suggestion is simple enough. Organize for life excellence! Begin by researching what unified efforts are already in place in your city. Perhaps a group of Christians is already on the move and all you have to do is join the party. If not, make a list of churches that you think would be sympathetic to the idea. You may want to meet with your pastor or other church staff for leads. Remember, this is an effort of lay leaders. Don't ask "full-time" Christian workers to join the committee (do ask for their blessing, however!). Try to represent the broad spectrum of churches in your community that have a deep commitment to the Word and a love for life. This may be threatening if you have never reached out beyond your church, but that is what the community of faith is all about—learning to lean on each other for the sake of the kingdom.

In some ways, you need to consider yourself a salesperson. You have to convince others that it is worth their time to get together with you—and many other unfamiliar people—to coordinate efforts on behalf of your city. Make as many contacts as you can by phone and then meet over coffee or tea with those who agree to be a part of the effort. Once you have a team in place, hold your first group meeting. We recommend that you choose your home—a neutral environment—for your first session.

An important rule to keep in mind as you organize: don't view this committee effort as a chance to push your favorite programs. Believe in the Family enough to build relationships around the Lord. Pray together as a committee that God will give you a vision for your city or town.

Once you have developed a base of mutual trust and respect, organize. This is the fun part! You get to plan together how you will influence your town for Jesus. Begin with reasonable, bite-size goals. No need to get depressed over failing to achieve unrealistic ones. You could begin by considering how to assemble a unified Sunday-school curriculum for all member churches—a curriculum that celebrates God's marvelous design of human sexuality and the benefits of following the scriptural pattern. As your committee manages to achieve its first small success, you are likely to garner the support of leading pastors for additional (and perhaps more creative) ideas for influencing your town.

2

A Fellowship of Parents

• • • • • • • • • • •

It's not easy to keep pace with the changes of our so-
ciety. Parents probably know that better than anyone else. The
desire to raise children with healthy values and the goal of
protecting them from destructive patterns in society is a force
hard to match. And yet parents do not want to push their children to separate unnecessarily from peers. The sense of isolation
and the burden of loneliness are extreme prices to pay and the
consequences can be just as damaging as unbiblical sexual
choices.

Parents are motivated to find means to nurture their kids with biblical notions of sexuality. But parents do not always find this to be a simple task!

If you have a knack for organizing, we suggest you form a "parents' fellowship." There are youth groups, Scouts, senior citizen clubs—why not focus on the parents too. The fact is, there's no more challenging task for a couple of human beings to face than the raising of their kids. It is just plain good sense to organize around this high calling and help each other along.

Begin by gathering together a small group of parents from your fellowship or church. Ask them to discuss the kinds of issues they are facing with their children. Identify the difficult areas where they would like some help. Become a resource group—share experiences, advice, failures and victories. After you identify the kinds of needs you face as a group, go after special resources to nurture each other in the task of parenting. Here are a few options you may want to look into:

☐ Attend (as a group) seminars that talk about family. If you are unable to find this kind of seminar in your area, ask your church to sponsor one. If you link up with other local congregations, you will be able to afford the cost of bringing special resource persons to your town. (See the "Resources" section of this book for some ideas.)

☐ Contact organizations that rent videos designed to help parents understand their kids' pressures during the teen years (see our "Resources" section for suggestions). There are videos that show the difficulty of resisting peer pressure, videos depicting the kinds of parties and events that attract youth.

☐ Organize parents' party evenings, where the focus is nothing more than loads of fun. If we do not play enough, we lose our sense of humor—the most vital tool in parenting.

☐ Take a step further—organize events for parents and kids together. These could be carefully planned events that are enjoyable to the entire spectrum of ages. It's a difficult idea to implement, but one that is well worth the effort. Children need to enjoy the company of their parents. If this is not a normal part of the younger years, parents will eventually be perceived as irrelevant and will lose the good influence they could have on their children.

☐ Our final idea here is for parents to attend events that are targeted specifically to their children's interests. This is a cross-cultural step for sure—real missionary work. Teenagers, especially, often get the message that parents write off their youth culture as childish, bad or just plain undesirable. This is read by youth as disrespect. Parents need to show their appreciation of the foreign culture of youth. For example, attend a rock concert. Parents do not have to "fake" their appreciation of the music if they don't like it. The goal is to show respect for their children and a desire to learn about their children's world.

Pray together as a group of parents that God will give you the ability to tenderly and firmly love your children; to avoid the trap of being above all an authoritarian "policeman" in their lives. Children need to know they have the freedom to grow and develop within certain protective boundaries. Parents need to help draw the lines in the right places.

19

3

Go to the Community

· · · · · · · · · · ·

You may find the courage to take the previous idea just a little further. If your small fellowship of parents seems to be making good progress toward supporting each other and being better at the task of raising kids, why not go to the local community—open yourselves to serving a larger group of people?

Here is what you do: put an ad in the local paper, church bulletins and town flyers saying that a local group of concerned parents would like to help other parents in the neighborhood. In essence; you are going to form a community support group for parents.

It is critical that you are clear with yourselves on your role with the support group: your job will be to serve the parents who decide to attend. This can be particularly difficult if you have a strong personality and an agenda that you feel all parents should understand! Remember, you are not trying to convert people to your viewpoint on issues; you are trying to nurture, encourage and support them in a difficult task.

This community support group can be as big as you have energy for. Several needs will surface. These become opportunities to meet people where they most hurt. Be careful not to extend yourself at first out of pure enthusiasm. You may ask the group what one project they would like everyone to work on first. You may be surprised at the answer. One group in Los Angeles decided there needed to be a good after-school recreation program to keep their kids off the street. A support group in Boston wanted to figure out a formal way to become a part of the classroom environment on a regular basis—they wanted to communicate the message that schooling was a parental idea, not just a governmental requirement.

Take advantage of city hall and the various civil organizations as you plan the support group. Once you move the idea of parental support from the church to the public, you are able to access a number of staff, dollars and support services that are "underused." It is in the interest of the city to have happy parents! Meet with the key movers and lawmakers and explain your plans. Ask for their advice on the best way to accomplish the goal and the people you should be contacting for help. Go to your local newspaper and solicit its help in describing your project to the public.

21

It is our experience that government and business want life to go well for the local residents. This gets people re-elected, it puts more money into the banks of local companies, it shrinks the prison population. But more important, these elected officials and entrepreneurs are just like us: they love children, they want wholesome families, and they are thrilled that someone is willing to organize local people around that kind of goal.

4

Organize a Concert

· · · · · · · · · · ·

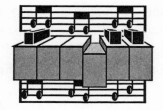

Being prolife means caring about the *quality* of life.
That includes getting our values straight. Perhaps you are not
comfortable with the cultural events in your town. You may feel
that the kinds of programs being offered will only put additional
strain on your youth to conform to contemporary patterns of
sexual behavior.

A town in the Midwest struggled with this question. They
wanted their youth to know that following a biblical lifestyle did
not require a total renunciation of their own youth culture. In
fact, they suspected that youth were falling away from Christ

because of this false separation that some clergy were insisting upon (clergy who just were not aware of the degree to which the generation gap blinded them to their own prejudices—if it's loud, long-haired and leather, it must be wrong!). This enterprising group of Christians decided to organize a contemporary Christian concert for the six hundred teenagers in the town. They researched the options and brought in a band that was louder, better and more metal than the town had seen to date. The youth (both Christians and those outside the family of Christ) figured they had died and gone to heaven.

Toward the end of the concert, the long-haired lead guitarist explained his love for Jesus and his commitment to follow Christ's standards of love, justice and purity. Needless to say, the impact was stunning. Christians had taken the lead in providing first-rate contemporary entertainment. And they destroyed the myth that following Jesus was an old-fashioned, fuddy-duddy concept.

To be sure, organizing the event had its risks. Would the older Christian community clamp down on future events and withdraw even more (they controlled the church life in this little town)? If so, youth who were currently in the church would have to suffer the consequences. And second, could the idea fly financially? The sponsoring committee decided not to risk unnecessarily. They called a committee meeting of the local youth sponsors and explained their desire to reach the youth for Jesus. They played samples of the music they were thinking of and were forthright with their need for financial help ("Would you sell tickets for us?"). These sponsors became part of the engine that made the event a wonderful success. The message to the youth was absolutely clear: you can follow Jesus with your whole heart and not be forced to put away the fun, acceptable parts of your culture. Youth outside the church heard the same message, and several have made commitments to Christ.

Plans are under way to repeat the concert every twelve months.

5

A Public
Presence
Against Abortion

• • • • • • • • • • •

We've talked about getting together with community
parents. We think you should also make the attempt to get
together with community leaders. This should be viewed as an
opportunity to build bridges with people who usually write off
the prolife people as "reactionary fundamentalists." We feel that
too often prolifers are sidelined simply because their agenda is
not "politically correct" or popular. As a consequence, an image
of prolifers begins to grow that is inaccurate and unfriendly. We
think community leaders ought to have the chance to form their
own opinion on the kinds of services you offer and the opinions
you hold.

In addition, this may be an arena where you can offer other alternatives to pregnant women who think abortion is their only choice. While you may not achieve as much as you'd like, you may prevent some abortions and influence some young women to not have future abortions.

A West Coast group of prolifers who operated a pregnancy clinic called a meeting with local physicians. They described the counseling the clinic offered to pregnant teens and parents, and spoke clearly about their conviction to treat all women with respect no matter their personal decisions regarding pregnancy. The physicians were quite charmed by these Christians and actually agreed to encourage all their clients to stop by the pregnancy center before proceeding with abortions. That simple meeting helped establish a bridge of trust and mutual respect which has now led to additional means of cooperation. Christians from the pregnancy center are referring clients to the physicians for medical counsel, and the physicians are referring clients to the pregnancy center for post-abortion trauma therapy.

Your city or town has several networks of leaders who touch people's lives in a professional manner—doctors, lawyers, therapists, police, teachers, local government (e.g., the mayor) and state or federal government (e.g., child protection services). As you begin to reach out to these different groups, you may discover that you yourself have plenty of prejudices to overcome! You will also discover that you have much more in common with them than your prejudices had allowed you to believe. Build these bridges of understanding with care. You are looking for means to serve needy people—it would be senseless to diminish your ability to serve because you are too stubborn to link up with people unlike yourself!

We often find the task of building bridges difficult because we want to "convert" others to our view. We sense that God has called us on a "holy crusade" and we fear we may have to compromise our message. But we are wrong. Francis Schaeffer urged Christians to grasp the opportunity to work with people of different theological views or motives—to be "cobelligerents not allies" as we acknowledge our differences and yet fight together against evil and work for a common goal. Our message is all too often lost because we unnecessarily alienate people. It need not be so.

II

Educate for Life

• • • • • • • • • • • • • • • •

6
Prolife Sunday

· · · · · · · · · · ·

Sundays provide a perfect opportunity to organize Christians, especially the local body, around a common theme. Every year as many as 100,000 U.S. congregations reserve a Sunday in May for the National Day of Prayer—a day for seeking God's intervention in the social, economic and political affairs of our nation. There is a growing movement of churches that now hold a special annual "Prolife" Sunday celebration. We suggest your fellowship or church join this groundswell.

Here are the kinds of elements you can organize into a Prolife Sunday:

☐ Create a special bulletin insert that summarizes some of the current issues our nation faces today with regard to being pro-life. Include a list of local organizations working toward these ends.

☐ Arrange for the sermon of the week to follow the same theme.

☐ If there are families in the congregation who have made personal sacrifices and commitments to ensure the quality of life for others, arrange for them tell their story to the entire congregation.

☐ Ask a local agency that works to serve the prolife vision to come to your church and share ways members can benefit from their services.

☐ Take a special offering to be split between an organization that serves unwed mothers and one or more single moms in need in your community.

☐ Put together a first-rate resource table at the back of the church for those who want to pursue the subject further. Offer free brochures as well as books or tapes to buy. The church might even establish a prolife library.

☐ Plan for each Sunday-school teacher to give a special lesson that week on the prolife theme. Subjects could be as diverse as how to adopt, what the Bible teaches about abortion, and caring for people who are unable to enjoy a sustainable quality of life.

☐ Advertise your special emphasis to the rest of the community. You may discover some needy or interested Christians who were looking for this kind of input. And you may even discover a good number of people who are not a part of the family of faith who want to explore these questions a little further. Be sure to include with the bulletin a response card or envelope for people who are looking for help in their personal lives. Perhaps someone attending the service is pregnant and does not have the information or courage to make good decisions. Others may be looking for information on how to adopt, foster or educate. It also makes good sense to include a brief survey requesting ideas for the next year's Prolife Sunday.

7
School Curriculum
· · · · · · · · · · ·

It is easy to feel that the secular system of education in North America is designed by people who intend to destroy the sense that Christianity is a viable system of belief in today's world. Too often the Christian faith is ridiculed without a fair presentation of its claims or history. (We must be honest about the fact that Christians sometimes engage in the same tactics when describing other nations or religions!) Encountering untruth and ridicule, some of us withdraw. The home schooling movement and Christian schools movement derive their popularity partly from this feeling of embattlement (this does not diminish the value of those movements).

Rather than growing as a forceful presence in the world, many Christian communities are giving up, admitting defeat. And they thereby lessen their impact in the world to the point where one could ask, "Where are the salt and the light?"

Hundreds of schools across the continent offer training in sexuality which only increases this sense that the public school system is "against us." Students in grades as far down as the fifth grade are at times encouraged to experiment sexually (as long as it's "safe") and to let go of traditional categories for sexual behaviors—categories which, they are taught, are nothing more than the values of earlier repressed societies. Children are left with no moral guidance for their sexual equipment unless the home and church provide an alternative biblical view.

Home schooling and Christian schooling do provide a strong biblical alternative. But Christian *parents* are supposed to train their children with biblical values—no matter what the secular educational system offers. The pressing question becomes, "What about the millions of youth who will never be home schooled by Christian parents or educated in a Christian school?" There lies the true challenge of reaching today's youth with a biblical standard of sexuality.

We need not abandon the secular-school kids to unbiblical views of sexuality. Entire school districts throughout the U.S. have embraced curricula that offer a biblical alternative in sexual behavior. Proactive parents led the battles at the school-board level, demanding that their point of view be represented in the curricula. As tax-paying citizens representing a sizable proportion of the school community, they insisted that the educational material include a more representative orientation. Virginity, sex within marriage and the dangers of sexually transmitted diseases were legitimate options and concerns and should be taught as dominant, acceptable options in our society today.

These visionary parents have trailblazed the formation of well-packaged curriculum that is now available at a reasonable price and perfect for the secular setting. We strongly encourage others to follow their example. Hundreds of thousands of youth are living better lives because of them. For more information, contact Teen Aid and Sex Respect, listed at the back of this book.

8
Sunday-School Curriculum
· · · · · · · · · · ·

Churches are an ideal place for learning about prolife concerns. Publishers create thirteen-week curricula aimed at all ages, so it is natural to slip in a learning series of similar length that helps us formulate our convictions and shape our lifestyle choices as they relate to the call to be stewards of life.

Unfortunately, there are few curriculum packages focused specifically on the topic of being prolife. But there are tremendous resources available to help create a custom package just for your church. If you are interested in pursuing this idea, this is what we suggest: Get the word out through your church bulletin that you want to meet with other members who are interested in cosponsoring a prolife Sunday-school class. You may be surprised to discover how many people have already been thinking about these questions, and you are likely to be introduced to materials that others have already tested. As a group, think through the best components to make up a thirteen-week package for your church. Here you have the luxury of making sure your program is suited to your people.

It makes good sense to actively seek the input of church members who have little exposure to prolife issues. They'll be more likely to attend the class when it is offered, because they sensed your genuine interest in their questions ahead of time. And you are more likely to become more sensitive to real needs. This will help steer you away from the tendency to "preach to" people about a subject for which you feel great passion. It is not our great ideas that matter. What counts is whether or not we have helped people inch a little closer to the kingdom and begin to adopt kingdom values.

Once you have decided on the basic structure of the class, review available resources. Look through the "Resources" section in the back of this book for more ideas. List your favorite materials (as a group). Don't forget "people" resources. There may be individuals in your community who have developed expertise in one of the areas you want to cover. It's always more interesting having a real, live person communicate the material. And if it is someone local, there is a chance some members of the class will pursue that person later for additional help. Many organizations will let you preview their videos if you explain that your church is trying to assemble a custom-designed package.

Our advice is that you not show material to the class that has not been previewed. You want each video to be a direct hit. Find out what your budget is and then make your final selections. Schedule the class into the church calendar and then find creative ways to promote it to the congregation.

If you have influence with a fellowship group on a nearby campus, design a shorter version of the same curriculum and offer to present it there. Get some of the students to help you adapt and promote it. Perhaps you could offer a three-evening program and then expand it later if some of the fellowship members wish to pursue the idea further. Another option is to tailor it for the campus in general and let the Christian students use it as an outreach opportunity.

9
Education on Reproduction

· · · · · · · · · · ·

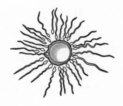

There is a lot of controversy surrounding the question of "sex education." It is important to separate *values* education and *physiological* education when we approach this controversy. Both are important and both should be taught. But they are not the same. The first helps us undergird our sexual lifestyle and practices with a biblical ethic; the second helps us understand our bodies and take charge of what happens to them.

Let's look at the physiological issues. It is quite astounding that in our modern day of technological knowledge, youth are so uninformed about the physiological specifics of reproduction.

To know your body and understand how it reproduces is to gain power over it—and to gain respect and wonder for it. The body is truly a miraculous invention of God.

These are the aspects of the topic which we suggest you communicate to the youth of your fellowship or church. We would point out that you may need to gain the permission of parents for each attending child. Some parents are not willing to allow others to have a formal role in sex education. (Of course, this education is continually going on in an informal manner, whether or not it is accurate.)

☐ puberty
☐ sexual intercourse
☐ conception and embryonic development
☐ delivery
☐ means of birth control
☐ sexually transmitted diseases
☐ myths regarding pregnancy, disease and birth control
☐ abortion
☐ rape

It is our opinion that we harm youth if we do not give them enough information to prevent them from foolish decisions. And we feel that our culture's open attitude toward sexuality makes an un- or ill-informed person all the more vulnerable to the misdeeds of others. If you need special help putting together a curriculum to train youth, see the "Resources" section in the back of the book, talk with other parents who have already gone down this road and consult with professionals in your community (therapists, educators, physicians).

And don't forget the parents who are a little uncomfortable

having their kids join a group session on this subject. Hold a parents' meeting (and even meet one-on-one when necessary) to discuss the kinds of resources they can use to educate their children in the privacy of their own homes.

10
Peer Pressure

· · · · · · · · · · · ·

Who can forget the crucible of the teen years?

Dress code. Hair code. Talk code. Cool code! Oh, the terror of being beneath the prevailing standards of what is "in."

There are clear reasons for the paranoia surrounding these apparently all-important issues: youth are busy defining their concepts of self and worth. They are going through the first conscious stage of establishing their position in society. Will they be accepted? Will they find approval? As they form their own sense of self, they are moving away from the security of Mom and Dad (steps of individuation) and yet curiously transferring that security to the peer group.

It is important to understand this pressure when appealing to kids to follow a biblical standard of sexual activity. Countless youth, when interviewed concerning their reasons for sexual activity, offer peer pressure as the primary reason. Not necessarily in those words, though. Instead we hear, "I didn't want to be the only guy in the locker room who is a virgin." "The other girls told me I was a prude for not having done it. They set me up with a jock from the football team." "Everybody's doing it. Why should I have to stand alone?" "At the party I was teased about being scared. I could see a few friends were having sex in the other room and so I guess I just gave in."

It makes a lot of sense to help youth understand how the self-image develops, how the sense of personal worth and value is established. It is important to know God's love for us, God's view of who we are apart from other people's opinions of us. When youth are able to link the desire for acceptance with the tendency to give in to peer pressure, they have a new kind of power over their lives. It is at this point that they are able to establish friendships with peers who hold values a little closer to their own. That is not being "cliquish"; it is being self-protective. Youth can be encouraged to develop a circle of friends where the sense of self can be developed in safety.

Sometimes it helps to make a link to other behaviors. For example, does it make sense to rob a grocery store with other youth because you will gain their acceptance? Or to damage your mind with crack? These parallel examples can provide a kind of red-flag reminder at times when the pressure is really on.

We have one other suggestion for dealing with this peer pressure: Organize events—and take your youth to events—that are culturally current. If there is a good rock concert in town, consider a youth rally that takes in the concert as part of the evening's activity. If some of the content is questionable, this is a great chance to talk it through with them and help them develop their critical faculties (not to lecture them on how evil all rock music is!). Youth culture is a dynamic thing; it keeps shifting. We have to keep our ears to the ground to stay in touch with *their* events and interests. And we have to be proactive in being a part of those interests, once we discover them. Kids are delighted when parents want to join them in having fun, rather than to criticize and disapprove.

When our kids feel they have to separate entirely from their own culture in order to be Christian, they just may one day say the price is too high and slip into activity they will later regret. And it may be due to our insensitivity to the peer pressure they are facing to be "somebody."

III

Focus for Life

• • • • • • • • • • • • • • •

11

Focus on
the Unborn

· · · · · · · · · · ·

No other area of the prolife movement has received as
much attention as the focus given to the unborn child. There
is good reason for this fact: That little child is entirely helpless
and presents to us the clearest picture of vulnerability to the
uncharitable designs of others. Both our conscience and compassion are stirred by this little life.

Our suggestion takes two paths: concern for that child's *right
to life* and concern for that child's *quality of life*. It is these two
poles of the child's life-in-the-womb that capture the breadth of
wholistic prolife care.

The Right to Life

Whether or not we are attracted to the *styles* of organizations such as Operation Rescue, we have benefited, as a society, from their strong *message* that hundreds of thousands of Americans believe it is morally wrong to terminate the life of a child in the womb. We cannot, as a culture, persist with abortions as though there were no ethical debate surrounding the practice. The church needs to continue this aggressive work on behalf of the unborn. There are several fronts on which such a ministry can work:

☐ At the political level, work and vote for candidates who have demonstrated by their lives a clear commitment to the child in the womb. One organization that focuses on this approach is JustLife. We have put their address in the "Resources" section. Join with other Christians in voting for people with prolife records and writing letters to your members of Congress and to the president. They need to know you are firm in your commitment to the unborn and that you believe protection for the unborn should be a matter of the law of the land.

☐ Do the same at the state level. It is fairly easy to meet with state politicians. Organize a group from your church or fellowship to get on their appointment schedules to discuss your concerns. Many times a politician will submerge his or her personal ethic in order to sustain the popular vote. Your presence could give him or her the courage to stay the course.

☐ Hold public protests at locations where abortions are performed (both clinics and hospitals). Organize prolife events in the town square or park. Bring in good entertainment and an articulate speaker to make the case for the unborn. Get a permit, and be peaceful and respectful.

☐ Write letters to the editor of your local newspaper or campus paper to protest abortion-on-demand.

☐ Help connect pregant mothers with adoption organizations. Many women choose abortion because they are unable to accept the responsibility to care for the child long-term. Your church or fellowship could advertise in the yellow pages under "Abortion Alternatives" or "Pregnancy." Have practical advice and help ready before people call. The offer of financial help with medical bills, a place to live until the birth and some emotional support may be the deciding factors in keeping the little baby alive.

Quality of Life

Hundreds of thousands of children suffer for their entire life outside the womb because of inadequate care while in the womb. Health specialists tell us that the critical formation of the organs and brain are determined almost entirely by what goes into the mother during pregnancy. (There are genetic issues too, but they do not carry the same broad impact as prenatal health care.) Here are a few suggestions:

☐ Your church or fellowship could link up with local pediatricians to offer free public health classes for pregnant moms. Offer classes on appropriate diet, exercise and child development in the womb.

☐ For people who do not have a health care plan that covers prenatal checkups, offer that service through your church. Many Christian physicians will grant several hours of free care per week. Your church could formally link itself to a number of physicians who would accept an agreed-on number of referrals from your church without charge.

☐ Make up nutrition packets for mothers who need a boost to their diets. Create these packets in consultation with a nutritionist and the local physicians or nurses who are working with you. Perhaps you can agree to provide a nutrition packet to each woman you refer for a free checkup.

12

Focus on the Homeless

· · · · · · · · · · · ·

Nobody has the exact statistics on homelessness in the United States. But the numbers are staggering however you read them. As many as four million people live in boxes, under bridges and in cars, abandoned buildings and our back yards. As many as one-third of them are children.

The lifestyle of homelessness is painful and degrading in every way. Facilities that we are accustomed to just are not there: toilets, showers, sinks, closets, stoves and fridges, to name a few. Bodies are vulnerable to the bitter cold, snow and wind, the drenching rain and scorching sun. Fever and disease are companions. Privacy is rare. And muggings aren't. Rape, robbery and "fun beatings" are part of the package. An alarming number of assaults have been discovered by police where well-to-do youth harm the homeless as evening sport.

We have several suggestions for focusing on the homeless:

☐ Research the homeless shelters in your community. It's good to know what is available for the homeless for the times when you cross their path. A hot meal and warm blanket on a winter's night can literally be the difference between life and death.

☐ Take a turn in staffing one of the shelters. Perhaps your fellowship group could agree to provide three people for each shift, one evening a month. The first team would take the evening shift, which would include providing a simple supper for the guests at the shelter. The second team would be there through the night. The third team would arrive with an early breakfast before the guests had to leave.

☐ If there is no shelter in your town, discuss the idea of establishing one as a cooperative effort among local businesses and churches. A shelter is best outfitted if it has beds, privacy, showers, food, entertainment and resource persons. The cost of running a shelter is not as high as one would expect. Get an organizing committee of folks who are willing to ask others for help; lots of people will volunteer once they understand what is required of them.

If you want help in establishing a shelter for the homeless, travel to a nearby community to see how it's done. There is no how-to-do-it manual, but you can learn a lot from observing others. We also suggest you contact Covenant House for advice and resources. They are the nation's largest center for reaching homeless youth. (Their address is listed in the back of the book.)

☐ You may find that a group of peers in your church or fellowship group wants to address the issues that lead to homelessness in your area. This is demanding and often frustrating work. But it is thoroughly Christian. Cooperate with the local agencies working with the homeless. See if it is possible to interview the homeless locally and begin to develop a plan of action for individuals. Some people have recently become homeless because they lost their jobs and therefore are unable to pay the rent. Others are runaway kids who are scared to return home. Some are developmentally disabled or emotionally disturbed and have been overlooked or rejected by loved ones. Work to find individual solutions that go beyond the shelter.

☐ Consider giving weekends or a vacation week to building homes for the homeless. An innovative organization, Habitat for Humanity, builds homes using volunteer labor from the community, volunteer labor from the person who is to receive the home and funds from a revolving building fund. The house is sold to the needy individual, interest-free over several years. Habitat is always looking for people who will launch chapters and building projects in their own regions. Habitat provides all the technical support, advice and encouragement you will need to make the ministry of building homes work in your neighborhood. Their address is listed in the back of this book.

13

Focus on the Prisoner

· · · · · · · · · · · ·

We have often been trained to view the prisoner as some kind of animal that is best locked away. Locked away because he deserves it and locked away because society needs to be protected from him.

There are a few such persons. But they are not typical of all prisoners.

Christians have reason to feel a unique bond with the prisoner. Our faith was birthed in persecution and imprisonment. Thousands of innocent men, women and children were thrown to the dungeons or the lions for no other reason than they publicly professed Jesus as Lord. And throughout the history of the expansion of the church, millions of believers have gone through the same unjust treatment. The New Testament calls us to care for the prisoner. This activity is equated with following Jesus. And in Matthew 25 the writer tells us that one way God will separate the sheep from the goats in the end of time will be to ask the question, "Did you visit those who were in prison?" Without twisting that passage into a theological prescription for salvation, we have to acknowledge that caring for the prisoner must be close to God's heart.

The life of a prisoner is marked by fear of other prisoners, fear of the guards, fear of the justice system, loneliness (absence of friends and family), impotence (inability to provide for family) and shame (the label of society). Many prisoners have a short record of crime that started with robbing the grocery store of $30 or stealing a stereo set from a car. Bad decisions and wrong behavior became the slippery slope to destruction. Christians understand this process. And we understand that most of *our* sins—equally weighty before God—do not receive the same harsh judgment in the eyes of society, nor do they separate us from loved ones, nor do they leave us frozen by fear. Our sins include malicious talk, impure thoughts, jealousy and envy, bitterness, the private affair, lack of compassion and a host of other "personal" sins. We are fortunate to come back each time to a Savior who loves and forgives us.

Society is not so kind.

We highly recommend volunteering with the work of Prison Fellowship as a means to begin caring for those in prison. This ministry, founded by onetime White House criminal Chuck Colson, is expert in its focus on those behind bars. The address is listed under "Organizations" at the back of this book. Or you may find a chaplain at your nearby prison who will be delighted to get some help with a good program he or she is already carrying on.

Services you might offer to prisoners include visiting them, visiting their loved ones, writing letters to them, writing letters for them to their family, donating used books and magazines, leading a Bible study, organizing a Christmas party—and, if you are qualified, counseling, legal help, and advocacy at governmental levels. Some individuals cannot contribute time at this point in their lives but can give money to a prison ministry.

14

Focus on the Developmentally Disabled

· · · · · · · · · · · ·

Our culture teaches us to quietly avoid people who are unable to care for themselves or whose manner is "embarrassing" to us. Even if we might like to reach out to them, we don't know how and so we look the other way.

The stress of building relationships with people who live with IQ limitations is real, to be sure. But we must confront ourselves with the question of how our behavior toward them reflects our convictions and values. Are they among the "least of these" who rank high in the tender heart of Jesus? Are they our brothers and sisters who, as the author of Corinthians says, need special care—part of the body nonetheless?

Most counties across the United States have homes for those who are unable to care for themselves. Sadly, a large percentage of these institutions are inadequately monitored, and the result is appalling practices that dehumanize those who live there. While some are well administered, at others the residents experience neglect, a poor diet, unsanitary conditions and lack of medical attention. Beatings, sexual assault and robbery are not uncommon.

The church cannot allow a "mass production" approach to caring for the developmentally disabled. It is our conviction that these facilities can be a wonderful help in our commitment to caring for such people, but not the chief answer or means to meeting their special needs.

Here are some of our suggestions:

☐ Assemble a group of Christians who would like to be a part of a special ministry to this special group. Be sure to bathe your initial sessions in prayer for compassion and patience. This is a demanding work. Research your county. Find out where the institutions are. Visit them. Become familiar with their operations. Ask for an appointment with each administrator, to communicate your interest as a group of local churches to care for those who live there. You may find resistance from some administrators if conditions are substandard. If so, you may be able to link yourself to relatives of those living there. Other administrators will appreciate your care and welcome your initiative and interest.

☐ Some places will welcome a friendship team which promises to come one Saturday afternoon each month to visit and play with the residents of a certain floor. You will find the residents very open and affectionate (prepare for lots of hugs!), and they will look forward to going for a walk on the grounds, playing simple games and so on. They are very sensitive to love; some who do not talk will gladly hold your hand. And some whose families never visit will be especially delighted when you come regularly, remember their names and give them a smile.

☐ At the advocacy level, you may discover that your local government and county officials are open to the idea of a Blue Ribbon committee whose job is to monitor these institutions. If so, assemble an expert team of therapists, physicians, pastors and parents to look out for the well-being of people living in these special homes.

☐ If you have an interest in caring at a career level, there are many social and medical programs designed to train personnel focused on these particular needs. If you are not sure whether this is your future but would like to test the waters, inquire with your local county officials about certification to inspect these facilities. Some states have a training program to license people to do part-time investigative work on the standards of these institutions.

We recommend that you support the wonderful Christian ministry L'Arche, focused exclusively on these needs. Their address is listed at the back of the book. And contact Joni and Friends (address listed in back) for materials and advice to help you in your service to the developmentally disabled.

15

Focus on the Children

• • • • • • • • • • •

The vulnerability of children provides a clear call to us to be completely prolife. The child in the womb lives in a secure environment, protected from inclement weather, poor housing, emotional abuse and much more. Too many children on the other side of the womb live a desperate life of fear, hunger, cold and physical abuse. For them, life outside the womb is not a welcome world.

Fortunately, most parents feel a special sensitivity to children. That God-given bond to love and protect the young is the source of our warning to not cross a mama bear! We suggest that you assemble a group of Christians who want to focus on the unique needs of children. There are dozens of ways to care for them. We list several below and suggest your group single out one or two for beginners. Perhaps over time you can expand your activities to include more.

☐ Research the special educational needs of youth in your region. Are you able to provide tutoring, class assistance or a resource learning center? Sometimes a community center already runs a tutoring program for kids whose families aren't able to help them with schoolwork or where academic motivation is missing. You can help one child, one evening a week, to keep up in school. That could totally redirect his or her life.

☐ Research nutrition needs. Are there ways you could supplement government initiatives to ensure a good diet and a sound mind?

☐ Research employment needs. Are the youth being adequately trained to hold a basic job? If not, are there ways your group could train them in skills that will help prevent poverty in the future?

☐ Research recreation needs. Are the youth pulled into gang and crime life because of boredom, inadequate supervision or lack of play facilities? If so, think through ways to ensure quality recreational facilities. Many kids are latchkey kids—their parents work all hours of the day, and the children are expected to care for themselves before and after school. Perhaps your fellowship could provide a special day care/recreation facility for these kids. Most church buildings are underused.

☐ As a group, be on the lookout for abused children. Too often they are unable to ask for help because of the threats of the abusing parents. Learn to identify abuse (see Sandra Wilson's *Shame-Free Parenting,* appendix A, for a list of indicators). And obtain information from your local government and physicians on how to provide help once you have clear evidence of abuse.

☐ Become a regular Big Brother or Big Sister to youth who do not have a mom or dad to model that kind of care and acceptance. You can do this informally if you know such a child or teen in your church or in some other way. Or you can sign up with the national Big Brothers/Big Sisters of America (address at the back).

☐ Research the need for fostering or adopting kids. This is obviously a much greater commitment, but a real need. There are more than a quarter-million youth currently in limbo in the U. S. These kids have no family that can or will care for them; they are shuttled between foster homes—wards of the courts. You can add stability, even for a few months, to a young life that is hurting for love. (Be aware of the emotional cost involved!) Even that temporary investment may show the child that *someone* thinks he or she is worth caring about. For a child who may have been given messages of shame and almost no affirmation at all, a loving relationship with you will be a lifeline.

16

Focus on the Elderly

Many traumas are faced by the elderly. This is a dif-
ficult and confusing stage of life for millions of people who used
to be lucid in their thinking, active in their physical routines,
passionate in their relationships and energetic in their pursuits.
Life was filled with opportunity, friends and loved ones.

Along the way these gifts retreated. And now the day is filled
with medical personnel, convalescent staff, pungent smells,
clinical rooms, immobility and loneliness.

Our American way of life has often been criticized by people
of other cultures who do not understand how we can so easily

lock away our elders. Whereas they bestow old age with honor and care, we appear to discard it. We are forced to ask what it is about the pursuit of the American Dream that turns loved ones into a nuisance. How is it that the love of money and pleasure crowds out the love of family?

These are difficult questions. But they are important ones and we need to be honest with them.

The truth is that for some families, making use of a nursing home is actually the most loving thing, even though it's a difficult choice for both the elderly person and the children/grandchildren. Talking with folks who have had to put a loved one into a home will give you insight into some of the needs that could be met by concerned volunteers.

Here are some practical ways to care for the elderly:

☐ Make regular visits to a rest home or nursing home near you. If possible, discover who does not have family nearby. These people are likely to experience the most loneliness. Drop in on several of them each time you visit. Just a few minutes' chat and a warm touch can be the highlight of the week for them!

☐ Take children to convalescent centers. The elderly carry fond memories of cuddling their young. And youth are a promise of life and tomorrow. Let the residents touch your baby. Have children tell stories, and let there be lots of hugs and holding of hands.

☐ Create special outings for the elderly. Because mobility is a problem with age, too often the elderly feel a dark curtain drawn about their diminishing world. For those who can still appreciate a trip but can't get out on their own, you could provide a wonderful treat by just taking them for a scenic drive and stopping for an ice cream. Or you could fix a simple picnic and take a group to a park that doesn't require much walking. Your church might offer this ministry to the elderly of the community as well as its own members.

☐ Consider allowing an elderly person to live in your home. Some medical programs that pay the cost of housing an older person in a convalescent center would also pay the cost of hiring a home health aide to make daily visits to your home to help with special cleaning and eating routines. Contact your state or local Department of Health and Human Services for advice on this idea.

☐ Research the standards and practices of convalescent centers in your region, assuring that the care provided is both legal and of high quality. This idea will require many hours and some professional know-how. We suggest you organize a coalition of local physicians who will take on this task. They are well acquainted with state and county regulations and are able quickly to recognize shortcomings. Provide them with some volunteer laypersons who can do much of the "go-fer" work.

☐ Involve the elderly in tasks when possible. Too often they have gifts to contribute but are ignored. Perhaps they have excellent counseling skills, historical reflections, the ability to pray regularly for those in need, or artistic gifts. We have seen it work in local churches where the elderly volunteered to serve on the 24-hour crisis or prayer line. You'll discover that some elderly folk have both the time and desire to assemble gifts for others—making quilts or toddler clothes, sorting and shelving in the church's food pantry, and so on.

17

Focus on People with AIDS

· · · · · · · · · · ·

It's tough enough to have a debilitating sickness that will kill you in the near future. Add to that the stigma of leprosy and sin and your life becomes a hell. This is the reality of hundreds of thousands of Americans who are dying because of AIDS.

The church failed when AIDS first became a reality in North America. Pompous preachers proclaimed the condition a plague sent by God to punish the homosexual and drug communities. One must wonder if God gave these preachers special insight at the advent of TB and polio. And one must wonder if the call to remove the log from our eyes has a better contemporary application today than the double standard held by most of us "normal" Christians—regular sinners who are fortunate enough to not be judged by God according to our many sins.

Our suggestion is simple enough. Begin with a group of people who believe God is nudging them to care for those with AIDS. Pray together that God would protect you from an arrogant spirit, and pray for merciful hearts and discerning minds. Once you sense you are prepared by the Holy Spirit, inquire in your region about AIDS victims. Are there centers where they live? Are there individuals in your school system or workplace who have AIDS? Find ways to be in contact with them. Perhaps you'll hear a friend mention having a friend with AIDS; ask to meet the person. Demonstrate that you simply want to offer nonjudgmental friendship.

And then begin the work of building relationships. We want to be clear this kind of work is fraught with the possibility of treating people condescendingly or "religiously." Avoid doing that, at all costs! Furthermore, you must be prepared to face rejection and anger from some who have experienced the judgment of the church and a cold reception by the culture. Your presence will be automatically suspect at first.

We recommend that your friendship be built on the desire to learn. To become equipped to spare others unnecessary suffering and pain. To become healed, yourself, of the prejudices and incompetence that prevent you from reaching out. This sort of attitude can build bridges of friendship and understanding.

Then you'll be able to contribute to a richer life for these people in the limited time they have to live. And you'll likely be able to talk honestly about life and death and faith. What you do with your new knowledge and your new friends is up to you!

18

Focus on the Dying

· · · · · · · · · · ·

As strange as this juxtaposition may sound, focusing on the dying is as prolife as it gets. To be prolife is to care for all the stages of living, from the womb to the tomb. And especially those final days when life is measured in days rather than decades.

For most people, death is both terrifying and desperately lonely. Even for Christians who look forward with joy to an eternity with Christ, there is still the painful passage from this life which separates us from our loved ones. We cling to both worlds and curse the choice.

There are many ways to minister mercy in the last days. You may be given the opportunity to be with a dying relative or friend at some point. Here are a few possibilities:

☐ Ask if there are any favorite stories, books or Bible passages you could read. Hearing the familiar can bring back many fond memories of childhood days. Even people who are not "religious" may find the psalms familiar and comforting.

☐ Perhaps there is some correspondence stashed away in a box in the attic somewhere. Inquire if you could read some of the letters out loud.

☐ And perhaps you could offer to write letters. At the point of death we are often faced with a need to bring closure to certain relationships or issues. Recording the words and making out the envelopes for a person who can no longer write could bring tremendous peace where a restlessness has prevailed.

☐ There may be certain relatives or friends who are especially important to this person. Ask if there is anyone in particular they would like to see or speak with. Arrange for a special visit or phone call.

☐ You may be able to offer some legal assistance if there is still the need for a will. If this is the case, ask around for an honest lawyer who has specific experience in wills and estates.

☐ Offer to pray. You want to be careful not to impose your religious desires on this bedridden person, but don't shy away from a straightforward offer to go to God in prayer. If the person is a Christian, this could well be one of the more precious gifts. And many others will be open to being prayed for too.

☐ Some people like Communion regularly and have no way to receive it. Offer to contact a pastor.

☐ If it seems appropriate, ask your dying friend to suggest other specific ways you could serve people who are dying. He or she may be pleased to have something useful to offer so close to the end of life. And you may have the opportunity to repeat this ministry several times over.

19

Focus on the Oppressed

· · · · · · · · · · · ·

God has called the church to demonstrate a special concern for those who are being unjustly treated. Many times in the Old Testament we read how God intends to punish the people of Israel because they oppress the poor. God looks upon those who are "bullied" by others in the same way a parent looks upon his or her child who is being pushed around by the school bully. And it should not surprise us. The Scriptures tell us that we were conceived in love. We are the children of God. And he is a God of great compassion toward the oppressed—but great anger toward the oppressor.

Too often the church has stood by silently while governments have oppressed their people. The innocent are defenseless and voiceless. If we do not speak up for them, no one will. In the prolife movement we understand that logic. We most often speak up for the voiceless person in the womb. It is exactly this kind of compassion that then moves us to speak up for those who are unjustly harmed outside the womb.

It is not always easy to engage in this type of ministry because we will often discover that as Christians we are the ones that need to do the repenting. That was not the case when we called for the protection of the child in the womb. We were on some kind of righteous crusade. We were talking about the sins of others. But as we begin to widen our focus of oppression to include Native American Indians, Mexicans, black South Africans and the like, we are faced with the disturbing reality that we have often been willing to go along with a kind of racism. And that is what most often makes oppression of others possible.

If you have not worked for justice outside the womb, you are entering new and probably unfamiliar territory. We have a few suggestions:

☐ Read a magazine that will help you to focus on these kinds of needs. We would suggest something like *Sojourners* or *The ESA Advocate*.

☐ Read a book that will begin to orient you to the biblical mandate for justice. Jim Wallis's *Agenda for Biblical People* is a classic.

☐ Join Amnesty International. Their specific focus is on political prisoners, government abuse and torture. In addition to adding to the membership, which gives the organization more clout when it confronts oppressive regimes, you will be encouraged to write personally to officials who are harming others. You *can* make a difference: an outpouring of letters has been documented in certain cases as being a major key in the release of a person from prison. The address is at the back of this book.

☐ Link up with a group of local Christians who are trying to work for justice. Ask God to help you be a shining light for his just standards as you advocate on behalf of those who experience unfair treatment regarding housing, employment or education.

20
Focus on Single Parents

· · · · · · · · · · · ·

There are several twilight years that happen upon the parents of young children. They walk around with glazed eyes, they snore during church, they never seem to catch the jokes, and they are easily distracted from regular adult conversation. It's a sure sign of sleepless nights and spent bodies. It is a good thing that in God's design, most children are born when the parents are still young.

Add to these normal stresses the hardship of being a single parent. The need to earn money, do all the house chores, chauffeur to all baseball games and piano lessons, organize smashing birthday parties, serve as room parent at school, do child care at church and model the perfect life of a Spirit-filled Christian—this is more than any normal human being was designed to take! Yet more than half of America's children are now cared for either by a single parent or no parent at all.

This is a great challenge to the church. And it is especially a challenge to the prolife movement that has made a strong case for God's design of the family. We cannot be at peace with our prolife convictions if we are not also finding ways to support those who are struggling to follow God's pattern for family.

We suggest that your church or fellowship group establish a committee of members who are committed to finding specific ways to soften the struggles of the single parents in your church and community. These do not have to be complicated or time-consuming. It is easy enough to take on small acts of kindness. Brainstorm together what special things you could do for single parents (and be sure to include single parents in that session). Here are a few of the ideas we have heard from single moms and dads:

☐ Offer to include their kids in your own family's activities on a regular basis. This lets the parent plan on a frequent, predictable stretch of sane time. Just like other parents, single parents salivate for an occasional hour alone.

☐ Offer to carry part of the load on certain celebrations—birthdays, graduations, baptisms and so on. An enormous amount of planning goes into these events; at times they fall by the wayside because the energy drain on the single parent is just too much. A party thrown by your family or by two or three of you from the church can be a treat for the child and the parent too.

☐ Invite a single-parent family over for dinner on a regular basis. That break from cooking and dishwashing and the conversation opportunities with another adult or two is a welcome treat, and the relief to the food budget is greatly appreciated.

☐ Offer your transportation whenever your kids are going to the same place as his or her kids. This may be school, sports or Scouts. Again, you are offering your friend some precious extra moments. If you are single, this is a great way you can help too. Simply ask a single parent if there is one regular car errand per week you could run—picking up a few groceries when you're shopping for yourself, dropping the child at an after-school event, or whatever is most helpful.

☐ If your family or church group holds a camping trip once a year, offer to link up with a single parent. You could share equipment, divide up food responsibilities and travel together. If you have children, switch kids to match ages. Or if you're single, become part of the single-parent family as an uncle or auntie for the weekend.

21

Focus on Children of Divorce

. . . .

Divorce is a tragedy. But it does not carry the same social stigma it used to. Thankfully, adults who have gone through separations from terribly abusive circumstances no longer have to hide from the public or church family.

No matter what the circumstances, however, divorce tears at our emotions. Children suffer the unfulfilled wish that Mom and Dad could change their ways and make amends. The loss of Mom or Dad has an immeasurable impact on the child, and the pain of losing the parent usually is felt far into the adult years.

We think that God has given some adults a unique ability to

focus in on the child of divorce. At the heart of this gifting is the ability to connect with the need for intimacy, safety, approval, physical proximity and tenderness. Children require this for the survival of their spirits. And they need plenty of it if they are to thrive as healthy, caring, integrated adults in future years.

We don't have a whole lot of specific advice to offer on this idea except to encourage those who have this kind of gifting/calling. Perhaps such folk could get together with other like-minded adults and pray for each other in this ministry. It is a high calling, in our view. Choose a family you already know, or ask a local social service agency if they know of a family which would like a new friend. Look for special ways to fill in the void left by the absent mom or dad. Be consistent in your uncle/auntie role; cut other activities from your schedule, if necessary, to make room for this ministry. A halfhearted approach will only reinforce the pain the child already feels by being half-parented at home.

Be sure to care for these children under the blessing of the single parent. Your role must not be read as a threat. It should mesh naturally with other family activities. The apostle James tells us that true religion is measured by the care of widows and orphans. We think that if he were alive today James would edit that comment to include the half-orphaned children who wonder why they are not good enough to be loved by both Mom and Dad.

22

Focus on Victims of Sexual Abuse

· · · · · · · · · · ·

We have to wonder at times if we are the new Sodom and Gomorrah. Just reading or watching the daily news shows us horrible examples of a very sick society that reduces women and children to objects of sexual fantasies. And it's not just the beasts and perverts we once would normally associate with such crimes against the human body and spirit. We read of fathers, mothers, clergy, police officers, teachers and physicians who violate the innocent. Indeed, we are told that most sexual crimes are committed by people whom the victims know.

Christians, above all people, should understand that God

created us as wholistic, integrated persons. In other words, we cannot separate the emotional from the physical from the spiritual. They each play into the other. We then should be acutely aware of the struggles faced by people who have been violated in such an intimate area as their sexuality, and worse yet, by those who they thought were trustworthy. There is a lot of difficult work ahead for people who have gone through these kinds of traumas.

We have a few suggestions:

☐ Make sure that your church or fellowship openly discusses these issues. Scores of people in the church pews are victims of sexual abuse but do not know they have friends who will walk through their pain and recovery with them. Churches should offer specific avenues for people to find healing. And these avenues must include access to people who are professionally trained in this area.

☐ Churches also need to raise the standard of Christian behavior in the congregation. Too many preachers give tacit permission to men and parents to abuse their wives and children. This can happen through sermons and Sunday-school lessons that elevate husbands and parents to near-gods. Nowhere does the Bible give parents and husbands permission to inflict physical or emotional harm on others. The word *prolife* implies respectful treatment of every living person. Prayer partnerships within the church can allow folks to hold each other accountable and to pray about the pressures that may cause them to lash out at family members.

☐ Churches can establish support groups for victims of abuse. It is likely that your church has several members who are victims. If you are in a small town, you may want to link up with other local churches for a united effort toward these victims of abuse. You could offer a discussion group where members look at Scripture to see how God regards the abuse victim, share their own experiences, then pray for each other. Using a guide such as *Recovery from Abuse* or *Recovery from Shame* (listed at the back of this book) will enable you to lead the group even if you're not an experienced teacher. Or a group might want to read and discuss a book such as *Released from Shame.*

☐ If there is none in your community, establish a crisis phone line that can quickly link up an abused person to the critical help. Women who have been raped need emergency care—physical, emotional and legal. So do children who have the courage to call a crisis phone number from school during recess and wives who gather up the courage while visiting a friend. Get legal advice before you start; advertise your phone number widely.

23

Focus on the "Unlovely"

· · · · · · · · · · · ·

Society's standards are cruel. From the earliest age, children learn to mock the child who does not understand the math lesson or who cannot kick a ball straight or who cannot see well or who has a speech impediment such as stuttering. This fact of society is particularly hard on those who have severe physical limitations from birth and those who don't match the cultural standard of beauty (Barbie and Ken).

The message of this cruelty, if we are to interpret it honestly, is that only certain models of God's creation are to be celebrated while other human beings are to be despised. This twisted view of God's loved ones is heretical and decidedly un-prolife. The church needs to counter this cultural heresy. We are all made by the special creativity and love of our heavenly Father; we do not need to be ashamed if we don't look or sound like society's ideal.

How do we help those who feel unlovely?

This is not one of those easier ideas where programs are available and special curriculum designed. This is, in our judgment, a sensitive area that calls for active discipling at the youth group level. Youth leaders need to model by their deeds that there are no favorites, that acceptance doesn't depend on physical beauty, that beauty is not based on the cultural queens. Parents need to exert the same sort of care and modeling as they sponsor youth events and teach Sunday school. Public discussion of these ideas is often too burdensome for those who are already suffering from a poor self-image. They feel singled out even though the direction of the discussion is in their favor. We know a youth pastor who pulls the offending "good-lookers" into a private session to discuss how they may be trespassing against God's standards and actually harming another human being. That youth group has a near-eerie feeling, it's so full of love for *all* God's people.

The bottom line is this: Any time we feel we can reject one of God's people, we have stopped being prolife. At that point we have no ethical basis to expect others to follow our anti-abortion agenda, because we are inconsistent in our position. And at a more frightening level, we have crossed God. We have violated one of his children.

24

Focus on the Family

· · · · · · · · · · ·

Yes, we couldn't resist borrowing a popular phrase.
The family is another of those contemporary situations where
special attention is critical. It is nothing short of a tragedy that
God's idea for a haven that can carefully nurture its members
and prepare young kids to thrive in life has for many become a
hell. The stories of abuse—both physical and emotional—and
the stress of survival in a society that seems to have lost its
moorings on the importance of relationships is overwhelming.
We would go so far as to suggest that we need to ask God to
work a miracle in our society today.

Obviously, entire books could be and are being written on helping the family today. We do not expect to add to those in this short space except to underline that being pro-family is a prolife concern. We cannot in good conscience demand the birth of children if we do not take care to ensure a good, safe, nurturing environment once they are born.

We suggest that your fellowship or local church put together a group of people who will focus on finding specific ways to serve the family. We want to be clear here that we are not thinking about the doctrinal kinds of issues that are preached to us regarding God's design for the family. Churches are packed with families that believe all the "right" things. And yet they cannot seem to survive the stress of modern-day living.

Get practical.

Announce to the congregation that you want to be a church that is sensitive to the areas where families are really hurting. Ask them to participate in an anonymous survey of all members to establish specific means to support the family. We would recommend that you put together a sheet of check-off possibilities and include a space for people to write their own response. Include the children in the process. Their ideas of need areas will be completely different, entertaining and even tragic.

Get help from a reputable family therapist to put together the questionnaire and then work with the therapist to debrief the results. This could be a painful process of discovering just how needy your church families are. It could be a highly informative process that offers just the practical kind of response you hoped for. Once you have a pretty good sense of the needs, publish a summary of the response for the congregation. Ask for volunteers to be a part of a working group to implement ideas. We think you will have more work than available time. People in and around your church may end up getting helped in some important and life-changing ways.

IV

Services
for Life

• • • • • • • • • • • • • • • • •

25

24-Hour Hotline

. . . .

Dan, a father in Austin, Texas, told the story of crisis in his family one evening: During dinner the son "spilled the beans" that his teenage sister was two months pregnant. The daughter, Laura, had intended to abort the child before her parents discovered the pregnancy. A fight ensued at the table where terribly mean and hurtful words were exchanged between parents and child. Laura left the house vowing to never come back. She did return, but all conversation ended. Dan did not know how to resume communication. He could not go to his church for help because they would judge him as a failure rather than provide desperately needed help. His daughter could not go back to the church fellowship because she was "living in sin."

Unfortunately for Dan and his daughter, they were not a part of a community of believers who understood failure and the need for mercy. The local church they attended was a significant part of their life—in fact, the center of their life. The idea of attending some other fellowship for help was not easy to consider. To leave their church would be to forsake the place of worship they had come to accept as the "true" fellowship of believers. This was especially true for Dan—and even though he was not receiving the kind of help one would expect from "true" Christians, Dan rationalized their lack of love as the consequences of his being a poor father. A sort of heavenly punishment.

Clearly, this family needed help to sort through some basic religious issues. Their view of God and the Christian body was terribly distorted. They really did live in bondage to others who exercised a supernatural power over them, not unlike the bondage experienced by many under the heavy hand of the Pharisees in Jesus' day. And it is precisely this kind of dilemma that calls for a way for Christians to find help without feeling they are abandoning God's chosen people or risking the loss of God's love.

Here is our suggestion. Gather together a group of people who have worked with parents and teens in trauma. Pray that God will unite you in a special love for these kinds of people in your city. Pray for a spirit of mercy, discernment and wise counsel. Then plan the program. Establish a phone line that offers free Christian advice and help to people experiencing difficult family circumstances. Place advertisements in the local newspaper, run a box in the yellow pages and, if possible, find a few Christian businesspersons who would sponsor small billboard advertisements displaying the emergency/helps phone number.

Decide how many hours a day your committee can cover the line. You may find plenty of good help from other churches. We recommend you attempt to make it a 24-hour service. The hours of midnight to 8:00 a.m. are easily covered by having the calls forwarded to a home. You don't have to stay up all night if you are on call—you only get out of bed if the phone rings during the night.

Be sure to familiarize yourselves ahead of time with the professional services in your county. Your goal as a committee should be to provide the most expert help available to families in crisis. A sensitive balance between prayer, encouragement and professional intervention is the kind of help Christians are uniquely able to offer. For some Christians who don't dare turn to their church, turning to this confidential phone service and finding nonjudgmental help may be a real godsend.

26
Pregnancy Center

· · · · · · · · · · ·

There is a growing movement throughout the United States to set up storefront pregnancy centers. These are the work of visionary laypersons who are willing to put a lot of energy and voluntary hours into the service of women and men in need. The services of these centers range from offering free pregnancy tests to arranging adoptions.

If you are able to volunteer about ten hours of your week to this kind of work and have organizational skills, we want to encourage you to consider this option. We are big believers in its value and effectiveness.

As with any large project, you are going to need a strong team of people who are motivated by a deep love for Jesus and a compassion for those in crisis. We suggest that you begin by bringing together a project committee whose job is to think through all the requirements to launch such a center. You may want a different team to implement the plan.

Members of the committee should include key clergy who have a history of helping families in crisis; professionals who understand adoption, fostering and family stress; medical personnel who understand the issues of emotions, embryonic development and testing; a lawyer who works with establishing new corporations; and Christians who have personally gone through the traumas of unwed pregnancies, abortions, adoptions and single parenting.

When the team is together, be sure to work on a solid foundation of prayer and biblical reflection. You are about to give birth to a ministry that will touch hundreds of lives. Approach it as holy ground and ask the Holy Spirit to equip each of you for this labor of love. There will be times of hardship and discord—the usual kind of squabbling and spiritual warfare that goes with running organizations. Once you sense a deep, mutual commitment to the idea of a pregnancy center, begin the planning. We suggest you include the following minimal services:

☐ Offer free pregnancy tests. Obviously you will need to find qualified personnel to administer them. Set up your center to include a nice bathroom facility and minimal laboratory.

☐ Provide counseling to pregnant women (and their "significant others") on the options facing them in their pregnancy.

Many couples choose abortion simply because they are unable to plan around the stresses of an unexpected pregnancy. You can help them think through their options and to link them with others who have made the same choices. Do not underestimate the power of community. The fact that you are there and willing to help through the entire term of pregnancy is a great encouragement. One single mom told us,

I was totally confused when I found out I was pregnant. My friend Elizabeth was firm in her opinion that I should not abort. But instead of focusing only on the wrongness and other negatives of abortion, she talked about the positives— the joy and miracle of a new life. She was excited about how good a mother she thought I would be and how I could be an example to others.

And she helped me deal with the future by offering her support and that of other Christians—both emotional and financial. Her strong faith caused me to take a closer look at Christianity and eventually to come closer to the Lord.

Elizabeth's sincere interest in me and my well-being, and her strong belief that abortion was wrong, affected me deeply. Today I am the proud mother of a beautiful five-year-old son. I've never regretted him for a second.

☐ Be familiar with the other services in town so that you can lead needy clients to additional services. These could include adoption and fostering, government assistance for food and housing, job skills development, job hunting and child support.

We would also recommend that you open the center at a minimum six mornings per week. This would require a total of twenty-four hours of volunteer time. You may want to add at least one evening, for those who work days. People are much more likely to avail themselves of your services (rather than skipping off to some other less wholesome service) if you have good hours. Advertise your service in local church bulletins, newspapers and the yellow pages. If you live near a university campus or high school, find ways to get into their publications.

If the idea of forming a new organization is a little overwhelming, start out as a committee of a particular fellowship or group of fellowships. As the organization grows, you can elect to become separately incorporated or stay linked to a particular church.

27
Marriage Counseling

· · · · · · · · · · ·

We live in difficult times. Considering the stress our society puts on families, it is a wonder that families manage to stay together at all. Prominent movie stars have gone on record with their view that marriage and family is a passage of life, not a secure station. It's something from which we eventually graduate. Recent surveys among college students have revealed an attitude that marriages basically do not work.

We need to hear this pessimism.

To be prolife includes a conviction that men and women can thrive together in an environment that is safe, healthy and emotionally secure. Marriage is God's idea. Even though our society is in a state of disrepair as far as marriage is concerned, we need to hold to our fundamental conviction that the institution of marriage is a good gift from God. To be sure, there are many myths that some families have carried forward over the years—the idea that we do not need help to communicate with our spouses; that if we set up a basic chain of command we will have a smooth-running military kind of partnership; that the family's struggles should be kept secret and never shared with other people. The Scriptures call us to be wise and humble. In marriage that may mean we need to understand how fragile relationships really are and be willing to go to people who have the skills to assist us in the development of healthy companionship.

Our idea is that churches should consider providing marriage counseling to both the Christian community and those outside the church. This is a demanding idea that will take plenty of coordination and long hours. But we are convinced that marriages cannot survive today without this special help.

There are several ways to implement this idea:

□ Hold marriage weekends. Some churches which do this discover that couples will open up to others' input into their lives. We want to be clear that we are not talking about the kinds of marriage weekends that simply rehearse doctrinal convictions on how God structured marriage. The need goes much deeper than that. We need help to communicate, to become intimate, to grow through the challenges of dashed expectations, to have courage to do the hard work of building up each other.

□ As a church, you may consider establishing a relationship with a therapist who would be willing to give an initial interview to any couple in the church who would like additional help. The church could subsidize the interview, paying half the cost. It's good to invest in the price of counsel.

☐ Churches could offer the same subsidy to married couples outside the church who feel the need of counsel. This may be just the sort of jump-start some need in order to get regular help. And it will be a "cup of cold water" given in the name of Christ.

☐ Offer specific seminars dealing with the points at which people are feeling the crunch in their marriages—economic stress, purchasing a house, changing jobs, relating to in-laws.

Clearly the options for assistance are wide open. We have only cracked the door. Above all, we want to encourage church leaders to be honest about their own need for others to help them grow stronger in their own marriages. Model to the congregation your commitment to the communication process, the hard work and the regular therapy sessions that prevent potential volcanoes and help repair the damage of earlier ones. Laypersons will not have to struggle with the stigma of receiving special help if they are able to perceive it as the choice of "professional" Christians.

28
24-Hour
Care Centers
· · · · · · · · · · ·

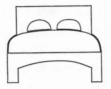

In our research for this book we asked parents for prac-
tical ideas to help them during these tough economic times.
Here is one of the surprising answers . . .

Many families are caught up in the job of surviving financially. It's not like the days when one spouse could work and the
other attend a little more closely to the children and home. And
it is not even a matter of both the mom and dad being away from
home in the daytime and then returning in time for dinner
together with the kids and a slow evening at home. Parents are
telling us they have to scramble for whatever work is out there.

There are a limited number of slots for employment. We are surprised to discover how many families split up over different work hours. It is not uncommon now to find Mom working from nine to five and Dad working the graveyard shift—or vice versa. Spouses and children are almost like the proverbial ships passing in the night. As a consequence, the few precious hours the family has together are stolen by the need for sleep—and life is in essence reduced to single parenting.

Some urban churches are asking what they can do about this contemporary conundrum. A few innovative churches have turned their facilities into 24-hour care centers. Parents who have to work split shifts are able to arrange a weekly schedule at the church to have their kids cared for while parents are taking care of family items such as shopping, fixing the car, talking to the banker, and trying to find a job with more reasonable hours. These churches have discovered that they are able to serve single parents, in particular, who have to work the late-night shift. These moms or dads can work assured that their tots are in a safe haven until the end of the shift. They pick their kids up on the way home, just as they would from a regular day-care center.

We have also heard that some families are helping moms who are on the graveyard shift. These moms drop the kids off at 10:30 p.m. in their pajamas and pick them up the next morning at 7:30 in time for breakfast. Adult volunteers "babysit" during the night while the kids sleep.

Nobody would consider this an ideal arrangement, but the alternatives are far worse. We need to become family to each other during these hard times. We do not have to accept these conditions as normative, but we surely want to put out the safety net to protect another family from becoming a homeless statistic or a government work case looking for foster homes because a parent was unable to provide during the rough stretch.

29
"Breather" Centers

· · · · · · · · · · ·

Here is a sensible, fun idea for reducing the stress.
Too many families go half-crazy simply because there is no regular, inexpensive release valve for the noise and energy that go
with raising young kids. This can be especially true of families
that live in crowded apartment buildings where there is little
outdoor space for running about.

Most churches are underused. Their classrooms, sanctuaries,
general rooms, kitchens and gyms sit empty most of the week.
We think it makes a whole lot of sense to provide a service to
church members (and others, if you have the energy and vision

to do so) where during the week for as many as three hours a day the church operates a kind of coffee shop/playroom not unlike a McDonald's or the sort of rec room you'd find in a mall. This is not a drop-off center where the mom or dad come back later. It's a drop-*in* center, a stopover that provides some relief and rest.

This is how you could arrange it: Call a meeting for parents who would like to be a part of this idea. Discover how many hours a week are needed, and which hours. Then begin to map out a schedule on a large blackboard until you find a happy compromise for the preferences. Perhaps you would begin with something as simple as two mornings per week. The idea would be to sign up child-care volunteers on rotation. Parents take turns being "on duty" with all the kids while the others are there taking a break—getting their minds off the kids for a short while, and having some pleasant adult conversation or just reading a magazine. If enough people join the scheme, each person would be on duty just once a month or so.

Find out what would be most refreshing to the adults. We think you'll want at least some tables and chairs with twenty-cent cups of coffee or tea. A small donut/cookie rack could be brought in each time for purchase at cost. Magazines, music and more could add the final touch. One church tells us that this center has become a primary place where young parents are not only recovering their sanity but finally beginning to develop friendships.

Add your own embellishments to this idea! One church built in an exercise room with weights and the like. Another holds a daily jazzercise session. If you are in a small church that cannot support this idea alone, reach out to other churches for a cooperative effort. You could eventually operate a full-time "breather" center that touches the lives of hundreds of church and nonchurch families each week.

30

Homes for Pregnant Teens and Young Moms

· · · · · · · · · · ·

Hundreds of thousands of our homes are virtually va-
cant. The kids have grown, and now there are two or three
bedrooms that do nothing but hold memories and collect dust.
An older couple or a widowed person rattles around in the empty
space. How about linking them to our commitment to being
prolife?

Each year thousands of pregnant teens decide to carry their
babies rather than abort. The decision regarding adoption or
single parenting may not be made right away; for now the major
life question is making it through the pregnancy. Kids who have

elected to stay pregnant tell of some of the stresses: Mom or Dad may use the growing tummy as an opportunity to "make a point" about how stupid and disobedient the girl has been; family members who disapprove of the decision may make life uncomfortable in the daily routine at home; peers may ridicule the teenager throughout her pregnancy.

The decision to choose for life is difficult enough. We need to help that child make it through a noble choice. Sometimes that means helping her temporarily relocate.

We are told stories of families who make their extra bedrooms available to these pregnant teens—homes away from home where the child is able to attend school in another district for six months and experience the loving care of adults who don't carry the baggage of family ties. The girl's parents are encouraged to visit at times, to go on outings together, buy clothes and give hugs. The pressure and embarrassment are reduced for everyone. Fortunately not all pregnant teens require this separation, but it's wonderful to have this option available for those who need it.

A vacant bedroom can also serve a single mom and her child, until she gets back on her feet. The months immediately after a divorce, separation, death, loss of job or unplanned birth can literally throw a single mom into poverty and a life on the streets. The extra cost of rent and utilities can be just the final nudge over the edge to ruin.

Why not actively seek ways to link up single moms with older folks who have extra bedrooms? The ministry goes both ways—each contributes to the life of the other. Organizing this linkage is easy enough. Get the word out at church that you are looking for folks to make their homes available. And get the word out to single moms. You may consider this a good ministry to people outside the church. If so, contact the local government department in your area that is in charge of child and family services. They regularly encounter single moms in crisis and would likely be happy to make your name available.

We recommend, though, that you form a support group for folks who are willing to provide this service. Taking someone into your home is time-consuming, often frustrating, sometimes even dangerous. Some hosts have been robbed of valuables, threatened physically and accused falsely. It's a tough job! Though they do it "as unto the Lord," these people need a group that will help them and pray them through it.

We want to emphasize the need not to "trap" needy people with your love. It is easy to judge others and consider ourselves slightly above their choices and consequences. The church needs to be a safe haven for pregnant teens and single moms, a place not of condemnation but of emotional support and warmth. Be careful not to offer housing as a means of evangelizing. Such an approach is dishonest and degrading. The Lord will provide natural opportunities to share your faith if your guest is not part of the Christian Family. Pray for sensitivity to those moments.

31
Nurturing
Network

· · · · · · · · · · · ·

Have you occasionally entered the state called Emo-
tional Overload? It's not an ongoing condition but a temporary
state related to the stresses and strains of life. You are just sure
that if one more car skids outside the house you will relieve it
of life with a square shot to the engine with your twelve-gauge.
Or if one more check bounces you will kill the bank manager
as a matter of principle.

Perhaps you can remember being visited by angels at a time
like that. There they came, out of nowhere. Friends from
church, the next-door neighbor, a coworker. Something about

their visit was perfect and refreshing. When they left, you had this uplifting feeling of being the focus of caring attention. It was your stories that everyone listened to, your washing machine hose that was repaired, your squeaky fan that got its screws tightened up. And they brought along your favorite muffins to boot.

No implied obligations when they said goodby. Just one of those goofy days when you are left feeling very warm about yourself and tomorrow.

God has gifted some people with a near-uncanny ability to focus on people at this level. It's as though they have supernatural insight into the trivial ways life overwhelms us. Their weapons against this emotional onslaught are duct tape, a plate of brownies, a Phillips screwdriver, needle and thread or an oversized hammer.

Their manner is unimposing, light, slightly apologetic and warm.

We think the church should recognize the ministry of this special group of ministers. Not that they should be organized into a formal force of mercy (that would work against their personalities), but that a simple, informal recognition be given to their nurture skills and ways sought to encourage them in their unique call.

Here are a few ways to do that:

☐ Let them know how their kind deed affected someone.

☐ Ask them from time to time to go after a specific need.

☐ Hang a bulletin board at the church where members of the congregation can post a specific need. Whoever has the time, ability and equipment to solve it simply removes the note and does the job. This will be a special help to the elderly and to folks with health problems.

You will discover that these folks are not in need of your administrative skill to do their work. They are internally motivated. You are just trying to connect them with special needs that may be out of their view. And don't make a public spectacle of their service. That kind of attention takes away their motivation and joy. Sounds biblical, doesn't it?

32

Intellectual and Artistic Stimulation

· · · · · · · · · · · ·

God created us with minds that require regular stimu-lation and an artistic side that needs to be nurtured.

When we are caught in the survival mode of life, these parts of us are denied attention. We do not always appreciate the impact of this loss upon our spirits, but we actually suffer malnourishment of the self in a way that leaves us feeling barren and two-dimensional. We have all seen the tragic regression of an intelligent, creative person. It's a flower that withers in the middle of a cool spring day.

Our suggestion is simple enough. We would encourage people

in your church or fellowship to actively seek means to bring overloaded people in contact with the creative world. Don't add to the overload: Choose something that is not going to bust the budget (or invite the individual to be your guest); also, be sure to arrange child care, perhaps group babysitting at the church.

☐ Plan a monthly outing to a local play or art show.

☐ Take suggestions for favorite bizarre movies, then arrange a video night to view one or two of them. Keep the popcorn and punch flowing.

☐ Get suggestions for stimulating discussions. Organize an evening around one of these topics where you bring in a funny, engaging person to carry you along as a group.

☐ Make a list of obscure and favorite music. Spend an evening around a CD player listening to Brazilian pipes or African drums. For a variation on this theme, have people bring favorite oldies; croon and howl away as you listen to Bob Dylan explain life and Elvis interpret love. Your kids will be sure you have left the real world.

☐ If you live near a university, look into its community catalog. You will often find an art class or history class offered as continuing education. The price is usually right and the hours are usually organized around work hours. Perhaps you could attend such a class as a group.

Particularly for folks who are lonely or who seldom get to think about their own needs because of family members who are leaning on them, these activities can bring terrific enrichment to life.

33

Home Work

• • • • • • • • • • •

If you own a company, this idea is directed toward you.

Many people are just unable to work outside the home. Perhaps there are physical limitations, young children, inability to secure child care or lack of transportation.

Thousands of companies throughout the United States have discovered that it may be less expensive to hire some work out to a person working at home who essentially functions as an independent contractor, rather than to hire more full-time employees. Certain costs go down: office space, utilities, staff management, insurance, taxes and certain benefits. Plus, you may have certain work that does not come in regular doses and is better served by an independent contractor.

Recognizing the business sense of this, some companies have helped a person—a single mom, perhaps—to set up a home office with the necessary equipment, and then written a work contract. A certain output per week is expected, but the number of hours and the specific hours are a function of the self-employed person. Here is a list of the kinds of jobs where companies are finding this to be a successful formula and where struggling parents are finding relief:

☐ Data entry
☐ Text entry
☐ Editing
☐ Desktop design
☐ Reading of manuscripts or manuals being prepared for popular distribution
☐ Assembly of small products
☐ Sewing
☐ Letter writing, secretarial services
☐ Collating mailings and stuffing envelopes
☐ Marketing phone calls
☐ Tabulation of surveys
☐ Catalog sales

We are clearly appealing here for a formula that makes business sense but also is sensitively aimed at the person who needs to work at home. The concept of a sweat shop is reprehensible and anything but prolife. We are optimistic enough to think that reasonable profits and economic survival can go hand in hand.

You may even want to go a step further with this concept.

There may be persons who have a skill you require, who would be willing to work as a regular employee of yours for twenty hours each week (from the home) and who need the benefit of medical insurance because they are not covered at present. You could ask the kingdom question: Should my business change its policies a bit to incorporate these kinds of needs into its mode of operation? We think that many of you will answer in the affirmative and discover a revitalized sense of mission for your corporation. The world needs people who have kept their Christian identity at the heart of their profit centers. That approach is biblical, is good for those in need, is good for the owner, and is good for a world that needs to witness kindness where calculators and cynicism are the rule.

34
Family Planning

· · · · · · · · · · · ·

The idea of family planning rings a lot of negative bells for some folk because the idea is sometimes linked with helping teens secure abortions or encouraging the use of birth control as a means to prevent pregnancy among teens.

We need to get beyond these stereotypes. The world's population is growing at a staggering rate. We will soon have a globe that is packed with ten billion people and an earth that is unable to support that many mouths. It is thoroughly a prolife issue to ask the question of how to keep the globe at a sustainable growth level. We venture the opinion that it is irresponsible of the church to avoid this debate.

Several issues need to be broached. We would encourage you to form a study group to investigate how you can become involved in this area of concern. Order materials from WorldWatch Institute and ask your local library for resources. World Vision International and Bread for the World are two good Christian sources of information. Here are some of the issues we face:

☐ How do we interact with governments (such as the Chinese) that are farsighted in their policies of population control but require abortions as a chief means?

☐ How do we interact with cultures (such as the Kenyan) where there is virtually no birth control in place and families easily reach fifteen members?

☐ How do we ensure that reliable, inexpensive, moral birth-control mechanisms are available to every global citizen who wants to have power over the size of his or her family?

☐ How do we find the appropriate balance—providing sexually active youth with birth control help while also calling them to a biblical standard of living?

We cannot allow ourselves to sit around mouthing simplistic slogans. The world is on a crash course toward poverty and violence because of overpopulation. If we feel the sharp need to end abortions-as-birth-control, we need to plan now for other means of birth control. If not, we will soon be living in a world where abortions are tallied by the several billion annually.

35

Community Development

We end this section of the book with an idea for people who are looking for a career in being prolife.

Community development is that science which asks the broad, integrating questions of a local community. It seeks to ensure a quality of life for local residents that is physically and emotionally healthy and promises a reasonably bright future. This is a noble pursuit, and, we would add, a Christian pursuit. There are schools that teach community development from a Christian orientation.

A typical community-development practitioner will want to

know if people have access to clean water, good medicine, basic education, family-planning resources, sanitary disposal systems and safe housing. Are they able to read and conduct contractual business without being vulnerable to corporate vultures? Do they have a clean environment policy, and are they safe from outside dumping? Are there adequate legal systems? Do the penal codes and rehabilitation programs protect the innocent and offer appropriate help to both victims and perpetrators of crime?

Those who want to make a career of community development can choose specific niches as different as teaching English, practicing medicine, building roads and bridges, practicing law, translating the Bible into the local language, developing sewer systems and lobbying the government. The call is to seek the welfare of an entire city—a call God gave to the Israelites of old as part of their community duty.

Get your local librarian's help as you research good community development educational programs. We mention two: UCLA has one of the nation's best Third-World programs. Eastern College offers the most innovative Christian version with a special emphasis on economic development.

V

Lifestyles for Life

• • • • • • • • • • • • •

36
Making Space for Feminists

· · · · · · · · · · · ·

Unfortunately, the rhetoric and energy of the prolife movement is all too often directed against feminists. Many circles operate on the assumption that to be feminist is to desire the destruction of homes, of babies in the womb, of marriages and even of the church. This view has developed largely because we are not listening to others, not opening ourselves to the possibility that we have much to learn from people who do not hold our convictions.

Feminists have had to fight for many rights over the centuries. Some of their agendas-of-old would not seem that radical now: securing the right to open a personal checking account, to purchase a home, to vote, to receive equal pay. To a great degree, our society has been structured in ways that do not allow women equal access to the wealth, power centers or leadership of our nation. And unfortunately the church has all too often been a force in denying women these kinds of rights. Consequently, feminists have often relegated the church to an irrelevant, if not evil, status, not unlike the apartheid government of South Africa that pushes down people who are not the "right color." Many women understand that evil, because they have been pushed down for not being the "right gender."

If we are going to impact our society for life, we will need to listen to the feminists. This can be difficult and threatening for women who have been taught to define their roles in life in contrast to feminist agendas—*I stay at home with the kids, I do not lead at church or in the public square and therefore I am a good Christian woman (as opposed to those feminists)*. Similarly, too many men establish their sense of worth by the role they fill—*I am head of my marriage and family, I am a church leader*—and so they are unable to listen to feminist concerns because to do so would threaten the very basis of their self-concept.

It is no easy task to get back to the basics and discover that our God-given self-worth is based not on what we *do* but on who we *are* (children of God, fearfully and wonderfully made). But then this is the work of discipleship. As you begin to listen to feminists, you may discover some biblical ideas that are missing from your own and your group's understanding. You may find yourself challenged to accept some of their values because they do indeed reflect a biblical worldview. And you may discover new friends in the work of being prolife.

Two excellent organizations wait to serve you if you choose to take on this challenge. They are Christians for Biblical Equality and Feminists for Life. Look up their addresses in the back of this book and ask them for help in building the bridges.

37
Tongue Twisters

· · · · · · · · · · · ·

In this section we have been speaking about building
bridges.

We need to mention the tongue. The Bible gives significant
status to the tongue. In fact, we are led to believe that there
aren't many things more powerful than that wiggling piece of
flesh. The tongue is capable of spreading fires, turning ships,
felling kingdoms, destroying children and ruining reputations.
In the book of Isaiah, chapter 58, God equates the need to
control our tongues with the instructions to feed the hungry,
clothe the naked, visit the prisoner and work for justice—all

prolife activities! We are instructed to put away the pointing finger and malicious talk.

Unfortunately too many of our prolife conversations fall into that negative category. We suggest here two ways we need to twist our tongues to conform more closely with our kingdom calling.

First, we must learn to be sensitive with our language.

Men in particular need to take care that their use of language does not force women to "translate" all the time. Here is an example from a typical Sunday service: "God loves all men." It is important to monitor our language to discover if we are using it exclusively rather than inclusively. If we are unable to appreciate the value of this concern, then we need to spend more time with women who have experienced that their gender translates to lower pay, fewer employment and education opportunities, fewer chances for advancement in a company and fewer options to establish a secure future that is not in some way dependent on the "good graces" of the opposite gender.

We have met too many women who have specifically decided *against* Christianity because the religious language of the church is full of masculine images—father, son—and short on feminine images—mother, daughter. We suggest your fellowship hold some fun Bible study sessions where you systematically search the Bible for feminine images of God. Incorporate these new finds into your regular language. Get help from Christians for Biblical Equality if you become stuck (address in the back).

Second, we must take care not to label people with unkind, untrue and humiliating labels simply because we do not agree with their values. It is too easy to fall into an "us-them" trap. We do it during the time of war. We label people we have decided to engage in battle *the enemy.* How else can we erase the sense that we are about to harm defenseless civilians along with armed soldiers? Similarly, if we can label feminists and pro-choice men with evil labels, then we do not feel the need to enter into relationship with them, to listen to them, certainly not to learn from them. Too often our prolife conversations, rallies and events are decidedly un-prolife because we engage in this form of unbiblical, malicious talk.

Here are a couple of action steps:

☐ Discuss the concept of careful speech with a friend or with your fellowship group. Study Philippians 4:8 and discuss how our thoughts about others affect our speech. Commit yourselves to making any changes you see are needed.

☐ Study Isaiah 58 and James 1:19-27. List some labels you have put on people which need to be dropped; then list some acceptable words you can use instead.

38
Time

· · · · · · · · · · · ·

Sometimes we are frozen in our commitments to make a difference because we just cannot seem to make the space in our regular routines to care for others. Perhaps we do nothing or very little because we wonder if our little contribution really does make a difference in the world.

We must be clear that the kingdom of God does not fit into a secular understanding of good works. We have been given the parable of the mustard seed to explain that our deeds for the kingdom extend much further than we would normally expect. Jesus told his disciples that if you plant a mustard seed (work for the kingdom) you would expect to find a small mustard plant grow. But instead we look out our window to the surprise of a tree large enough to perch birds. And so it is with our efforts to be prolife. God will take our small deeds of faith and multiply them. This is the economy of the kingdom.

We suggest you begin by taking inventory of your available time. Could you put ten minutes each week into working toward prolife concerns? Ten hours? Whatever amount is reasonable for you, it is good to have a goal. We have listed several ideas in this book that could take anywhere from ten minutes to a lifetime. We suggest that you link up with a friend who wants to make a difference and together you select two or three ways you can take action. By involving a friend you will be able to reflect on your progress with someone else's input. And it is so much easier to follow through on commitments when you don't have to go it alone. In time, you and your friend may even decide to expand your circle to include others. Just be sure to adopt a reasonable pace.

Here's an idea that will almost *save* you time. Organize a "90 Minutes" weekly do-something dinner: Form a group of three to ten people who will eat together on a certain evening every week. Make it a very simple standard meal of bread, cheese and soup. Take turns providing the meal. Use the time to listen to and discuss a Bread for the World article, or to each write a letter to Congress as suggested in the JustLife newsletter—some practical task. Take turns providing the action program for the evening, including the writing paper, stamps and envelopes. In stead of each person's spending time cooking and washing dishes at home, you'll have a good time, learn something and

127

accomplish an important task—all in an hour and a half.

And be sure to lighten up! God does not stand over us to scold us for not doing a "perfect" job. God sees our heart and delights in the fact that we want to make some kind of difference.

39

Question the Rat Race

• • • • • • • • • • • •

One of the biggest enemies of life is the rat race. We are driven, it seems, to destroy ourselves by sprinting through life with little or no reflection along the way. Too many people have the same message to offer others at the end of their lives: "Slow down and focus on what is truly worthwhile." And it is no surprise that time spent with family is one of the most-mentioned areas where people express regrets.

It is our opinion that in the Western world today we need to ask some very fundamental questions about our lifestyle. Do we have a basic drive to become upwardly mobile, to acquire, acquire, acquire? What is the source of that drive? What do we expect to gain because of it? In other words, what benefits do we see or what models are we copying which hold us to that pace? And a more difficult and honest question needs to be asked: What are we losing in our fast-moving lifestyle? Who are we harming by it? What message goes out to our loved ones because of it? What does it say about our Christian orientation?

We cannot be prolife if we are consumed by personal pursuits. We all need to take inventory of our wild chase. Here are some of the questions that will help us draw a more accurate picture of ourselves:

☐ Are we hospitable? Does our life allow us time to be host to other people, bringing tenderness and friendship to their lives?

☐ Do we find that we are regularly listening to (vs. talking to) others? People who are too much on the go don't have time for two-way relationships.

☐ As we reflect on the previous few months, do we see clear ways in which we've been able to touch people in need? Are there people near us who would actually consider our friendship to have been a saving point in some of their recent traumas?

☐ If we have children, do they clearly feel the freedom to walk into our circle of activities? Are they being pushed aside regularly? *(I'll talk with you later. Not now, honey. Hurry up and get it over with!)*

☐ Do we find that we are able to practice Christian community with other members of the church? Do we sense a deepening of relationships or have we just not been able to squeeze it in? We are not talking about being busy in programs. We are talking about developing community.

Being prolife is not essentially being in favor of certain ideas or holding to certain ideological positions. Being prolife is about living. If you're in the rat race, make some changes.

40
Growing for Life

· · · · · · · · · · ·

Being prolife is a process. We are constantly learning about the world. We are disciples of Christ, which implies we want to grow. We want to walk in Jesus' footsteps. Our exposure to new needs can be a little threatening because we may discover that our new understanding requires us to let go of certain viewpoints, to be willing to let go of the security we gain from the "in" group.

But then, we have the King to help us in this challenging task!

Frankly, we fear that much of the prolife movement is not

about growing with Jesus. Too often it seems to be about shouting our currently held opinions at people who disagree with us. We would like to call for a level of activism that is always "upgrading" itself, always looking to improve. Here are a few suggestions on how to do just that:

☐ Arrange family outings to places that are unfamiliar to you. Perhaps this will include convalescent centers, prisons or hospices for the dying. As a family, focus in on the people there and ask yourselves what it means to be prolife to them.

☐ Perhaps you could take a slightly braver step and arrange a family vacation to include a three-day stopover in another culture. Most white Americans are within a day's drive of ethnic urban communities, Native American reservations or the Mexican border. Our prejudices have a hard time thriving once friendships and real people are involved. You could phone a black or Hispanic church in your city or a city near you, asking them to tell you honestly whether you'd be welcome at their service, explaining that you don't know much about them but want to learn. Ask them to *help* you take steps of growth. Or, ask your pastor whether your denomination has a specific ministry you could contact in your own city or the city you'll be visiting on vacation.

☐ Watch videos, read books and magazines, go to the movies. You are sure to gain a much better understanding of how to make a difference. We would also encourage reading materials and watching movies that contradict our own views (or at least that challenge our ideas). Most of us activist types do not really believe that the "other side" has legitimate and reasonable positions.

Be intentional in your willingness to change your views as you take in more knowledge. You may be surprised to discover that you have held racist views of another ethnic group. Make a mental note of the need to avoid jokes that put down these groups. Be open to improving your understanding of others. This process requires faith and courage, but it is the only option for people who claim to be prolife.

41

Spend for Life

· · · · · · · · · · ·

Money and time are very similar commodities: there
never seems to be enough of either! So again, we need to
budget.

We suggest you link up with a friend and ask him or her to
hold you accountable for a small weekly commitment to financ-
ing prolife concerns. You will discover that no matter how small
your donations are, you'll feel the satisfaction of making a difference. Ministries are operated by real live people and their
efforts to help those in need just will not happen unless we give.
Our experience is that once we begin to give, we find ourselves

cutting back on some personal items in order to give more. It's natural to give. That is how God created us.

We would recommend that you divide your giving into three areas:

☐ Growth: Spend money on a few magazines, books or movies that will increase your ability to be prolife. We have listed several possible resources at the end of this book.

☐ People: Ask God to sensitize you to individuals who would benefit from a little financial boost. Always make the gift in a way that affirms the person's dignity. Perhaps you could give it over a cup of coffee or make a nice card expressing your respect and best wishes for the person. Sometimes getting it to them anonymously is the best way.

☐ Organizations: We have listed several organizations in the back of this book. We would recommend that you look for ways to spread your donations over the variety of prolife concerns. This will keep you on several informative, motivating mailing lists and help prevent a tunnel-vision kind of activism. Perhaps you will want to include a pregnancy center, a justice ministry and a relief organization on your donation list.

42

Pray for Life

. . . .

We have kept prayer for the last item in this section.
There is always a certain hesitation to include this kind of idea
when looking at making a difference in the world. At times the
attitude prevails that if you cannot do anything *real* to help, at
least you can pray.

We strongly oppose this belittling of prayer. We do not claim
to understand the mechanism of prayer. It is a mystery to us that
God designed a way for us to implore him—for things he already
deeply feels! But such is the case. And we can testify to the fact
that we have seen the circumstances of people change—mirac-

ulously so. Only the most bitter of cynics has not occasionally whispered *thank God* from the heart.

Prayer can be very personal: *God, please help me to change my attitudes toward prisoners and victims of AIDS.* Or, *God, I'm willing to change the way I spend my time and money—please help me take the baby steps.*

Prayer can be specific: *God, please heal our friend Jonathan.* Or, *God, help Susan choose for life, and we pray that her boyfriend will encourage her too. And, God, please give the Supreme Court wisdom and a sense of your justice as they decide on the current prolife issue before them.*

Prayer can be general: *Oh God, we just don't understand why so many people have to suffer from hunger and political oppression. Would you please visit this world with your kindness, mercy and justice.* Or, *God, we do not understand earthquakes, famine, volcanoes, floods and war. We pray you will comfort the millions of families around the world who are suffering through these tragedies.*

For some reason God is moved by prayer. Someday we're going to ask him to explain that to us!

Make a commitment to both individual and corporate prayer for life. You may set a goal of one minute per day alone with God, praying for life. And perhaps you could convince your Sunday-school teacher to open each class with three or four community prayers for life.

The Scriptures tell us in Matthew 9 that when Jesus was overwhelmed by the pain of hurting people all around him, his response was to talk with his Father. We think it is a good idea to follow Jesus' lead.

VI

Advocate for Life
● ● ● ● ● ● ● ● ● ● ● ● ●

43
Corporate Policies

. . . .

It is not a simple task to create a profit-generating company that pleases all its employees. Too often employers trying to make the company survive—a goal that is clearly good for the workers—harm the workers in the process. And some-times employers' greed impedes good work policy decisions. Just ask those who were laid off by corporate giants (ostensibly due to the recession) what they think of the fact that their former CEO still draws a salary and benefits package of several million.

We want to encourage employees and employers alike to ask what their companies would look like if their employee policies were made with a basic prolife orientation. These are some of the things that we feel should be talked through:

☐ Medical insurance. People who are paying their own medical insurance costs are paying almost twice the amount they would have to pay if they were on a group policy carried by the employer. There are creative, ethical ways to narrow this gap by establishing a staff-funded corporate plan.

☐ Child care facilities. Every company needs to deal with the fact that kids today lose out because of the requirement for two paychecks. Companies should consider establishing an on-location day-care facility for toddlers and babies. Too much money and too many hours are spent by parents trying to arrange for child care. Employers should realize that their staff would be much happier and much more productive with this kind of service available nearby. And parents would happily share in the cost of the program.

☐ Maternity leave. Companies need to be proactively prolife by defining a leave policy that does not harm the employee or her family. We have to allow for the birth of our children and the security of a place back at work after the recovery period.

In a day when some fathers are taking on a major part of the child care role, companies can assist with this by working out an equitable arrangement for paternity leave as well.

☐ Gender equality. Too many companies are filled with men at the top and women at the bottom. It may not be a written policy but it is clearly a practiced policy. Men and women alike need to protest this double standard and work with management to create a just policy and practice. Management needs to realize it may be wasting a prime resource if it is keeping women from

141

using their potential or losing capable women to other companies.

☐ Employers would be more open to adjusting their benefits package if there was the sense that employees were pulling for the future of the company. It is too easy to enter an antagonistic relationship. We suggest that employees look for ways to actively work for the long-term health of the company. Offer to talk with top managers about how you can do this. There may be ways to share profit based on performance. The point here is simple enough—managers and employees need to become long-term partners with a genuine commitment to working together.

44

Public Policy

· · · · · · · · · · · · ·

Fundamental to the American experiment in govern- ment is that we, the people, operate the system. It doesn't feel that way very often, but that is mostly a function of our having withdrawn and allowing the professionals to "take over."

Public policy is simply that body of rules that comes out of government—those rules that set the moral and legal requirements on how a nation is going to conduct its business and social life. Christians need to take an active part in forming public policy. We have the privilege to work for bills and laws that reflect a biblical vision for our nation. To be sure, this is the art of compromise at its best, but to remove ourselves from the process is to withdraw the salt and light.

Here are a few suggestions for those who want to impact public policy:

☐ Subscribe to important newsletters that will help form your understanding. Christian organizations that specialize in this arena are Evangelicals for Social Action, the Family Research Council, the National Association of Evangelicals, JustLife, the Association for Public Justice and the Institute for Religion and Democracy. As you read, you will find that at times they hold opposite views on bills that are pending in Congress. This is part of the fun of being Family! (Addresses are listed in the "Resources" section.)

☐ We suggest that you work specifically at the local and national level on the following issues: Work for a fair employment policy in the United States that includes maternity leave, medical insurance and child care. Fight the social ills of abortion, pornography and violence in the media.

☐ At the local level, advocate fair housing practices for low-income people. The idea of a slumlord is real and alive. These unscrupulous persons elevate profit over humane living conditions. Some innovative judges are now requiring slumlords to live in their own apartments as part of the sentencing. Study local budgets to determine if services such as schools, recreation, parks and libraries are fairly distributed to lower-income neighborhoods. If not, advocate on behalf of the poor.

☐ Meet with government officials and explain your grievances. Be courteous, specific and professional. You put the government in office; your voice deserves to be heard. Sensible elected officials will listen carefully if they hope to have a career in politics.

☐ If you are motivated enough to do research, try to learn about the different people living in your community who are underrepresented. Link them up with policy formers to initiate legislation for passage.

☐ Bread for the World organizes letter-writing parties aimed at flooding the nation's capital with mail regarding a specific piece of legislation. The idea is very effective and has moved millions of dollars to fund programs for the poor—programs hailed by both sides of the House.

45

Organize a Public Protest

· · · · · · · · · · ·

There are times when our convictions do not become part of public policy or of the staff manuals of major corporations. We still hold deeply to our conviction that the laws need to change because of their impact on people. At this point we are faced with the option of public protest. Some personalities thrive on this kind of ministry! It must be done carefully, in the spirit of "speak the truth with love."

The largest contemporary example of public protest is the Operation Rescue program designed to block abortion clinics. Some Christians favor this strategy; others are not so sure. Either way, the work of OR has been the single-largest form of notice served to the nation that abortion is morally unacceptable to a great number of its citizens. Lawmakers cannot ethically ignore this "voice of the people."

If you have the stomach for this approach to ministry, we encourage it. Public protest was the chief tool of the nation in the sixties when citizens were saying "Enough!" to the unfair treatment of blacks. Christians who opposed the killing of thousands of civilians in the Vietnam war took the same approach. Protest is a legitimate tool of democracy, and we think Christian citizens should employ it as often as seems appropriate. We believe that protesters should be careful to exercise the fruit of the Spirit both in public and private and to be consistent so they will avoid—or at least not deserve—the label of hypocrisy.

Besides protesting at abortion clinics, here are a few additional ideas:

☐ Stage protests at hospitals that do abortions. They have been missed by the focus on clinics.

☐ Stage protests at the homes of public officials who are unwilling to give a fair hearing to your prolife concerns.

☐ Organize sit-ins at government buildings. The Sojourners community in Washington, D.C., organized one in the rotunda of the nation's capitol. Several hundred members of the group prayed the Lord's Prayer in unison while being told over megaphones that their prayer was illegal. They were arrested and carried off to vans while finishing the prayers.

☐ Organize sit-ins at businesses that practice unfair policies toward the poor. It makes for a great media grabber and gives free air time to your (well-thought-out, well-articulated) views.

147

☐ Organize marches around government buildings regarding unjust laws or illegal arrests. In Los Angeles several Christians joined Palestinians to protest the illegal detention of Arabs who were accused of terrorism. Due process had been denied these seven men and women. The federal judge released the prisoners and lectured the federal agents on the Constitution. And some interesting alliances were established between Muslims and Christians.

VII

*Resources
for Life*

• • • • • • • • • • • • • • •

46

Magazines and Letters

· · · · · · · · · · ·

Over time it's easy to settle into a few favorite publica-
tions—and miss the rest. We have listed several here that we
think will be of value to you in the pursuit of a balanced, biblical
prolife agenda. You may find some of them at your local library—or be able to convince your library to carry them. If not,
they're worth the subscription price.

Bread for the World
Frequency: monthly
Cost: $25
Published by BFW
802 Rhode Island Ave. NE
Washington, DC 20018

Context
Frequency: quarterly
Cost: free
Published by World Vision
  Canada
6630 Turner Valley Road
Mississauga, Ontario
Canada L5N 2S4

ESA Advocate
Frequency: 10X per year
Cost: $20
Published by Evangelicals
  for Social Action
10 Lancaster Avenue
Wynnewood, PA 19096

JustLife News
Frequency: bimonthly
Cost: donation
Published by JustLife
P. O. Box 7165
Grand Rapids, MI 49510

Journal of Christian Nursing
Frequency: quarterly
Cost: $17.95
Published by Nurses
  Christian Fellowship
P. O. Box 1650
Downers Grove, IL 60515

Priscilla Papers
Frequency: quarterly
Cost: comes with mem-
  bership—$20
Published by Christians for
  Biblical Equality

380 Lafayette Road, S., Suite 122
St. Paul, MN 55107

Religion & Democracy Report
Frequency: 10X per year
Cost: $25
Published by the Institute on
  Religion and Democracy
1331 H Street NW, Suite 900
Washington, DC 20005

Sojourners
Frequency: monthly
Cost: $30
Published by the Sojourners
  Community
P. O. Box 29272
Washington, DC 20017

Together Journal
Frequency: quarterly
Cost: $12
Published by World Vision
  International
919 West Huntington Dr.
Monrovia, CA 91016

Urban Family
Frequency: quarterly
Cost: $11.80
Published by the
  Perkins Foundation
P. O. Box 40125
Pasadena, CA 91104

Washington Watch
Frequency: monthly
Cost: donation
Published by the Family
  Research Council
700 13th Street NW, Suite 500
Washington, DC 20005

WorldWatch
Frequency: bimonthly
Cost: $20
Published by WorldWatch
  Institute
1776 Massachusetts Ave. NW
Washington, DC 20036

47
Organizations

· · · · · · · · · · · ·

There are several organizations that will help you in
your commitment to be prolife at every level. They will differ in
their views on some specific ideas; read and decide for yourself.

Remember to contact all the organizations listed in the previous section. The groups listed below are in addition to those names.

AIDS Resource Ministry
12488 Venice Blvd.
Los Angeles, CA 90066

Amnesty International
322 Eighth Ave.
New York, NY 10001

Big Brothers/Big Sisters
 of America
230 N. 13th St.
Philadelphia, PA 19107

Covenant House
P. O. Box 2973
New York, NY 10116
Toll-free advice line:
(800) 999-9999

Feminists for Life
811 E. 47th Street
Kansas City, MO 64110

Habitat for Humanity
Habitat and Church Streets
Americus, GA 31709

Joni & Friends
P. O. Box 3333
Agoura, CA 91301

L'Arche
1701 James St.
Syracuse, NY 13206

Prison Fellowship
P. O. Box 17500
Washington, DC 20041

48
Videos
• • • • • • • • • •

We list below four organizations that have put hun-dreds of thousands of dollars into creating videos aimed specifically at youth. Topics available include peer pressure, AIDS, pregnancy, single parenting, broken families, racism, abortion, dating, sexual intercourse. All four have catalogs; ask to preview material before renting or buying.

Josh McDowell Ministries
P. O. Box 1000
Dallas, TX 75221
(800) 222-5674

Respect, Inc.
P. O. Box 349
Bradley, IL 60915
(815) 932-8389

Teen Aid
North 1330 Calispel
Spokane, WA 99201
(509) 328-2080

InterVarsity Video
P. O. Box 7895
Madison, WI 53707
(800) 828-2100

49
Movies
· · · · · · · · · · · ·

There are a few recent secular releases that sensitize the public to specific needs. We think they are expertly made and are a good basis for discussion. (Some have ratings of R.) Below are our favorite choices.

Awakenings
A true story of people in a catatonic state

Children of a Lesser God
A portrayal of a hearing-impaired woman

Clean and Sober
A painful study of addiction

The Fisher King
A look at homelessness

My Left Foot
A true story about cerebral palsy

Radio Flyer
A difficult portrayal of child abuse

These films are likely to be available as videos after they have left the theaters. Get several friends together to watch and discuss: What new insights did we pick up about the people, their condition, how the world around them reacts? Is there someone we know who faces a special challenge and whom we could help or encourage? Is there a local program in our town that needs volunteers?

50
Books

· · · · · · · · · · · ·

We have selected a wide variety of books that cover
various aspects of prolife concerns. Each is introductory and will
point you to additional resources.

Campolo, Tony, and Gordon Aeschliman. *50 Ways You Can Feed
a Hungry World.* Downers Grove, Ill.: InterVarsity Press,
1991.

————. *50 Ways You Can Help Save the Planet.* Downers
Grove, Ill.: InterVarsity Press, 1992.

Grant, George. *Third Time Around.* Brentwood, Tenn.: Wolge-
muth and Hyatt, 1991.

Hayford, Jack. *I'll Hold You in Heaven.* Ventura, Calif.: Regal, 1986.

Hull, Gretchen Gaebelein. *Equal to Serve.* Old Tappan, N.J.: Revell, 1987.

Nouwen, Henri. *In the Name of Jesus.* New York: Crossroad, 1989.

Ryan, Dale & Juanita. *Recovery from Abuse.* Life Recovery Guides. Downers Grove, Ill.: InterVarsity Press, 1990.

Shelton, Chuck. *Voiceless People.* Global Issues Bible Studies. Downers Grove, Ill.: InterVarsity Press, 1990.

Sider, Ronald J. *Completely Pro-Life.* Downers Grove, Ill.: Inter-Varsity Press, 1987.

Swaby-Ellis, E. Dawn. *Sanctity of Life.* Global Issues Bible Studies. Downers Grove, Ill.: InterVarsity Press, 1990.

Swindoll, Charles. *Sanctity of Life.* Dallas, Tex.: Word, 1990.

Truman, Bryan. *Basic Human Needs.* Global Issues Bible Studies. Downers Grove, Ill.: InterVarsity Press, 1990.

Wallis, Jim. *Agenda for Biblical People.* San Francisco: Harper & Row, 1984.

Wilson, Sandra D. *Released from Shame.* Downers Grove, Ill.: InterVarsity Press, 1990.

_____ . *Shame-Free Parenting.* Downers Grove, Ill.: InterVarsity Press, 1992.

Wood, Glenn, and John Dietrich. *The AIDS Epidemic.* Portland, Ore.: Multnomah, 1990.